113

IN SPITE OF MYSELF

By Winthrop Sargeant

IN SPITE OF MYSELF

JAZZ: HOT AND HYBRID

GENIUSES, GODDESSES AND PEOPLE

LISTENING TO MUSIC

IN SPITE OF MYSELF

A Personal Memoir by

Winthrop Sargeant

1970

DOUBLEDAY & COMPANY, INC., GARDEN CITY, NEW YORK

B
Sargeant

To Jane
The Lady at the End of the Book

FOREWORD

The following document was written nearly twenty years ago, with no thought of publication—merely to try to help clarify certain things to myself. Now that I am allowing it to be published, I have become conscious that it is a sort of auto-biography—a highly subjective example of the species, perhaps best described as a case history. During the intervening years I have changed considerably. I have long since made my peace with the art of music, and I enjoy writing about it, though it still seems necessary to me to write occasionally about other subjects in order to preserve my contact with that large part of society which takes no interest in it. This seeming necessity may be imaginary, and a residue of neurosis. But I think that it also has a genuine side. I am interested in the world I live in, and that world contains a great many things besides music.

As I read over what I wrote so long ago, a number of things about the document strike me as wholly foreign to my present state of mind. One is the extraordinary desire for power that runs through almost every page. Another is a note of self-pity that is the aftermath of psychoanalysis. I have let these stand, though they are no longer part of my view of life. I am now sixty-six years old—officially counted among the aged who are entitled to such things as Medicare. The awful struggles recounted here now seem a bit unreal to me, and the tremendous egotism with which I have written about them a bit excessive. That poor former self that was mine never experienced any major tragedy, any real pain, as pain is generally regarded. It was born too early to take part in the First World War, too late to take part in the second. It never knew real poverty, real illness, or real material deprivation of any sort. It was a thoroughly bourgeois self, with bourgeois ideals, puritanical despite its erratic behavior, remarkably old-fashioned even for its time, and prone to a reserved sort of bohemianism purely through the circumstance of education as an artist. Yet it managed to create its own devils and its own sufferings which, as I read about them today, seem to have been fully as tragic as the real tragedies of normal people. I sympathize with this former self. But I am glad that it is no longer mine. It might be reasonably asked why I am publishing this curious account at all. I am a writer, and it is a piece of writing. I suppose that some habitual exhibitionism is involved. But, beyond that, I am doing so in the hope that the few people who suffer from afflictions such as my past ones may possibly gain something from reading it. I have come to know, and to know about, a considerable number of musical infant prodigies. All of them, without exception, have felt betrayed by their parents, and nearly all have found their adult orientation to the art a highly disturbed one. To them, at least, the story will be familiar.

Yet, the strong hostility toward my parents that is expressed here seems to me, today, somewhat out of proportion. I owe them a great deal, and if my upbringing and education have been somewhat eccentric, that fact has not been entirely disadvantageous to me. Moreover, no one can be blamed for his neuroses. They are a matter of fate—often of one generation's small madnesses reacting against those of another. Never, I am sure, did my parents seek deliberately to inflict on me the sort of life that I have led. Their motives were generous enough. And, since this document was written, I have come to take a more tolerant view, as if we were all small children groping our way—they as well as I. Whatever bitterness is contained in what follows has since evaporated. I am no longer dissatisfied with my lot in life. I rather like it. Moreover, both my parents are long since dead. My father died in Paris while I was at work as an orchestra musician in New York. My mother lived to be a very old lady, and died more recently in San Francisco.

w. s.

CONTENTS

I   11

II   39

III   85

IV   133

V   171

VI   213

VII   239

Some years ago, I—outwardly a fairly successful journalist—encountered a psychological experience that convinced me for the moment that I was at least partially insane. It was one of those occurrences usually referred to as "nervous breakdowns." Its immediate causes seemed clear enough on the practical and conscious level. I had been, for some time, a fairly important writer—off and on a roving correspondent—on the staff of *Life* magazine. My work, at the moment, kept me in New York, writing articles. At that same moment, the editor of *The New Yorker*, William Shawn, offered me an additional job as a weekly columnist, a job that could be carried on at night and on weekends. I believed that I could manage both jobs at once, since my work at *Life* occupied only part of the daylight hours. And there was a considerable financial inducement—the two jobs, done together, would increase my income by a good deal. Now, *The New Yorker*, as everyone knows, is a sophisticated magazine that demands a polished style. Much of what it prints is regarded as literature rather than journalism. Accordingly, I spent a great many anxious sessions at the typewriter trying to polish my style. At the same time I was conscious of a debt to the editors of *Life* for their generosity in permitting me to take on the extra job, and I was determined that it should in no way interfere with the efficiency of my regular work for them. The two magazines between them took up virtually every waking hour of a seven-day week. I was, quite obviously, overworking myself. Why? Was my motive simply greed? I do not think so. I have rarely in my life written anything from a purely mercenary motive. The satisfaction that I take in writing for its own sake has always been the primary reason for what I do. The explanation was something else. I was not a particularly happy man. Like many others I have known, I was using work as a drug, as a means of escape from what is vaguely known as the "real world." As it turned out, there were other explanations too, but overwork seemed the most conspicuous one. At any rate, there came a point when I was unable to continue. I should have recognized the approach of this point long before it arrived, but I did not. I have, all my life, been a highly disciplined person. What I set out to do, I did. My recognition of the state I was in did not occur until I was already beset by severe psychological symptoms, and even then I gritted my teeth and carried on. Finally my symptoms became so acute that any attempt to write, or even to think consecutively, was accompanied by a curious combination of terror and rage —emotions that got progressively worse. I had to telephone Mr. Shawn to tell him that I could no longer continue at *The New Yorker*. And, worse still, I found myself unable to go on with my work for *Life*. I took to my bed, where I was cared for by my wife, and where, in many a dim, groping way, I tried to figure out why this odd state of mind, which seemed all out of proportion to its rational causes, had come upon me.

There were other, less obvious causes of my condition too. I had recently returned from a long sojourn in India, where I had been observing, interviewing, and writing articles. There, I had contracted a serious case of infectious hepatitis, and, unaware of my physical condition, had gone on working, drinking a good deal to dampen my symptoms (which I attributed to the climate, to mental disturbance—to anything but the real source; in fact it never occurred to me to consult a doctor until I was back in the United States again, and when I did I was put in a hospital for several months to recover). I have mentioned mental disturbance. I had experienced mental disturbance before in far places, and at home too. It usually presented itself as attacks of anxiety which I quelled by the force of will, by thinking about something else, by "snapping out of it," as the saying is. I have all my life been subject to fits of depression or anxiety, and have been accustomed to coping with them in one way or another. In trying to explain them I have stumbled on various theories of my own derived from reading about such things in books on psychology. The thought has often occurred to me that I am mentally unbalanced. Despite the gregarious requirements of life as a journalist, I am a very withdrawn person. I can tolerate the society of others up to a point, but then I must be alone for a while in order to collect myself. The "others" seem to occupy a different world from the one I live in. I can communicate with them, interview them, analyze them as an icthyologist analyzes a fish in a tank, and write about them fairly expertly. But I cannot remain for long periods in their world. If I try, I feel like a deep-sea diver whose supply of air is beginning to run out. I must return to my own subjective environment where I can calm myself and prepare for the next dive.

Why this should be so, I had no inkling at the time I am writing about. True, I had led a remarkably solitary life for long periods, and I had often found myself in conflict with the world inhabited by most people. Perhaps, I thought, my condition approached that of a paranoid or a schizophrenic, or both. I seemed to discern two different planes of reality—the "secure," unthreatened, calm plane on which I lived when I was alone, and the dangerous, disturbing plane on which I met all others except perhaps a few close friends and my wife. It was on this disturbing plane that I earned my living, except for the part I devoted to the actual process of writing. Writing had been a part of the safe, subjective plane. Like any typical journalist, I had hundreds of acquaintances. But I had few close friends, and those I had were odd ones. One of them, a Hindu Brahman named Sarat Lahiri, had died recently, having drunk himself to death after his wife left him. Another was a reformed alcoholic who suffered from acute mental disturbances. It was among such people that I really felt at home. The *Life* magazine office with its gaiety, and its hordes of pretty researchers and quite agreeable editors and writers, was—except for an intimacy with one or two individuals—a place where I carried on a masquerade—outwardly gregarious and happy, inwardly shrinking. The outward gregariousness required a considerable amount of drinking to sustain it.

While I lay on my back in bed, trying as best I could, with the help of such readings in Freudian psychology as I had absorbed, to identify the causes of my affliction, I pondered over and over again my curious alienation from reality. What, after all, was reality except a convention agreed upon by sane men as a compromise between their differing views of it? There was no reason to suppose that any two men experienced precisely the same "real world." No two men were precisely alike. Their views of the "real world" were, in all probability, like the leaves of a tree, all of which are similar in general pattern, but no two of which are exactly identical. Maybe the "real world" didn't exist, or existed as a manifestation of something else, as my Brahman friend Lahiri had believed. Still, it was obvious that most people lived on the plane called "reality" and experienced no serious mental disorientation in doing so. And it was equally obvious that I was accustomed to feeling safe only on another plane. Evidently I had constructed for myself a substitute world, or part of one. It was a highly intellectual world, made up of abstract ideas, sensations of a personal nature, aesthetic enjoyments, landscapes through which I moved, meditations which were a source of imaginative flights that pleased me—and writing. This world contained no people except myself, not even my wife or my close friends. It was, as I have said, a safe world.

Usually, as I lay in bed, such pondering on the metaphysics of my identity ended only in a wave of numb terror that blotted out all thought. The notion occurred to me that I might slip completely over the border of rationality and become a simple madman—one who might have gone around buttonholing people on the street and saying, "You know, the fact may very well be that you don't exist." But I wanted something else—the ability to come to terms with that strange "real world," with its attractive women and its apparent satisfactions. The attractive women seemed particularly important. Not that I had never known such women. I had had two marriages and many affairs. Still, the attractive women appeared, somehow, to be connected with the "other" world.

At this point enter Mephistopheles. I say this, because, as I look back at my plight, it seemed to me at the time that I was acting out the myth of Faust. Like him, I had found scholarship and thought an empty pretense. I was forty-five years old, and I had never fulfilled my youth. Mephistopheles was my psychiatrist, on whom I called in the last stages of helplessness and depression. He did not appear in a puff of smoke in response to an alchemistic incantation. But there was plenty of aboriginal smoke and alchemy in the primitive reliance on stark, helpless fear and emotion that drove me to seek his aid. Rationally, I had always had certain objections to Freudianism, which I had regarded as a sort of witch doctoring. I still think of it that way. But rationality had failed me. I was forced, for the first time in my life, into something resembling an act of faith. And faith is something that exists on a primitive level of the human mind, having to do with intuition rather than reason. Like Goethe's Faust, I took a chance. I threw away the world of intellectual certainty, and demanded entrance into the dangerous world of desire, impulse, fear, and what the theologians call evil (a word I hate because of its popular use by prudes, but which has a special dynamic meaning in theology). The new world turned out to be the world of human contact. (This development would probably have surprised nobody but me.) Here, Mephistopheles began to teach me many things that I had, in my intellectual pride, remained ignorant of. He gradually broke the artificial shell of my dead world of scholarship, and forced me to reveal to myself the human being inside it. This human being did not by any means conform to the ideal of what I had previously thought I ought to be, and often deceived myself that I was. It was shown to me that what I considered my most generous and admirable attitudes were often mere masks for the most primitive impulses toward murder and other forms of destruction. It was demonstrated repeatedly that my past picture of myself was loaded down with a vast weight of hypocrisy, that I had deceived myself by mistaking cowardice for lofty detachment, and that my outward show of serenity and good nature was merely a method of asking forgiveness for a deep hostility toward my fellow men. Mephistopheles showed me myself, and I was not pretty. But I was human, and I began to develop human needs, impulses, and emotions.

One of the most obsessive of these emotions was loneliness. This surprised me greatly, as I had spent a considerable part of my adult life in solitude—at work or reading—and had never consciously experienced this feeling. Probably it is more accurate to say that I had never *allowed* myself to experience loneliness. Some powerful need for self-sufficiency had forced me—even in adolescence—to turn to solitude and work rather than to people for comfort. I considered people to be dangerous and untrustworthy, while work occupied that special place—the perfect world that I was completely in control of. At any rate, I very early formed the habit of concentrating on some idea or object—some book or some piece of writing or musical exercise—whenever I was alone, thus shutting myself off even more completely from the outside world. Hadn't all the romantic stories about artists, poets, and philosophers stressed this notion that creative activity and the world of ideas was the one dependable refuge of the intellectual man when everything else went wrong? How false these romantic stories were! Or, at any rate, what a false basis they made for a way of life. There is nothing wrong with a certain amount of solitude, or with treating the world of ideas as an occasional refuge. But I had so imprisoned myself in this world that I was afraid to leave it, even momentarily. Scholarship, to me, had become a narcotic. It had replaced friendship and most forms of social recreation and entertainment. It had replaced practically all human emotion.

I am, at this point, of course, describing only one facet of a rather complex personality. Naturally, I had had considerable contact with practical things too. I have always had to earn a living. And there were dozens of other factors which contributed to my peculiar isolation from society, factors which had to do with the vicissitudes of my career, my rather unsatisfactory relationship with my family, and so on. I shall take these up later on. My ingrained need for self-sufficiency and my fear of the real world did not, in fact, succeed in isolating me completely. There were chinks in the shell, and occasionally the human being inside would revolt desperately. These revolts usually took the form of extreme attacks of anxiety, which I quelled again and again by main force. I had, then, no understanding whatever of their causes, for I had never really taken the trouble to understand myself. I attributed them to some vague disturbance in an unbalanced mind. It occurred to me that possibly my grip on sanity was being maintained by a more or less continuous and deliberate effort of the will. I practically never mentioned my condition to anyone, even to my closest friends or my wife. Once or twice I tried to explain it, but gave up in dismay after finding that no one understood. I had the feeling of being two people— one, the disciplined, placid, and kindly personality I exhibited to the world; the other, a sort of mad demon who continuously threatened me, and whom I kept in forceful subjection during practically all of my waking hours. I was desperately afraid of this demon. At times he seemed about to overwhelm me. In my psychological naïveté, I considered him to be evil, and my external, placid personality to be good. He was the demon of impulse and desire, and most thinkers had held that impulses and desires were dangerous and had to be tamed. The battle against him was so stringent and severe that the impulses and desires took irrational forms, which only confirmed my notion that he was evil and a threat to my mental security.

I will not dwell on these irrational desires here, because they are clinical rather than easily explainable. They were mostly of "compulsive" character, and are well known to psychiatrists. Suffice it to say that the most obsessive and powerful of them were sexual fantasies, and that they made my relations with women extremely complicated and difficult. I am not, even at this writing, completely clear about my very ambivalent relation to women. But certain irrational attitudes are plain enough, and all of them seem to involve conflicts. In general, I am very fond of feminine companionship, but I regard every feminine companion as a potential trap—as someone who is likely to put me under an obligation which I do not wish to fulfill. Therefore, I tend, as a rule, to move on from one companion to another. I am also very much afraid of my own tendency toward dependence on women, and the moment I find myself mothered and taken care of, I become frightened and restive. It seems to me under these conditions that I am losing my capacity for coping with the world, that I am becoming weak and helpless, and that I must make a break in order to prove to myself that I am independent and tough enough to weather the stresses of life. If I do not make this break, I tend more and more toward chronic invalidism accompanied by extreme fits of depression. I tend, on the whole, to divide women into two categories—those who are potential friends, and those who attract me sexually. I seem never to find the friendly woman sexually attractive or the sexually attractive women friendly. The dilemma that this attitude creates is obvious enough. It associates sexual attraction with fear and hatred, and friendship with impotence. The various escapades that this state of mind has involved me in would be a fit subject for humor, if it were not for their serious and tragic side. For the fact is that I cannot get along without women, that I am fascinated and obsessed by them, that the mere sight of a pretty woman on the street fills me with both desire and anxiety, and that I find the satisfactory consummation of the sexual act an almost incredible joy for which I would willingly sacrifice practically anything else in life. Sex has to me the obsessive character that alcohol has for the alcoholic, or opium for the drug addict. It seems to be the remedy for all psychic conflicts, and the great escape from all problems of life. But it isn't really the satisfactory escape I imagine it to be, because it involves its own train of anxieties and difficulties. Obviously I have not yet solved the problem of my relations with women. Perhaps I shall never solve it. So much for sex—for the moment, at any rate. During my period of withdrawal from the real world, I regarded it as a dangerous and unbalancing impulse—something that broke out of bounds occasionally and ultimately had to be suppressed for the sake of my peace of mind. Since Mephistopheles has appeared I am attempting to study it and cope with it directly. But, so far, I have not learned how to do this.

While Mephistopheles demonstrated that I could feel lonely, and began to show me that women were people instead of dangerous chimeras, the area of activity involving my work continued to exhibit a mass of confused and resentful symptoms. This is a complex area. It involves a curious scattered career which started as that of a violinist and infant-prodigy composer, and passed on into a furious but completely frus-

trated ambition to be a symphonic conductor. It passed from
that into a phase when I was actually a musical scholar and
critic but wanted to be a general journalist and struggled to
get away from music as though it were a poison. From there
it went on to a final escape from everything connected with
music, when I became a writer on politics and other general
subjects for the magazines. Then, finally, the appearance of
the second nervous breakdown at forty-five, following an attempt to do a column of music criticism for *The New Yorker*
magazine. After this breakdown the mere sound of music
created extreme anxiety. There was also an extreme reluctance
to write about music. It is only recently that I have been able
to listen to music at all, and even now, I resent it as if it were,
in some way, a source of betrayal and injury. I still feel deeply
that I regret having had anything to do with the art, that
somehow my life would have been more satisfactory if I had
never learned how to play, write, or write about, a note of it.
It seems to me like a great, threatening inferno, or a sort of
cage, which has cut me off from everything valuable in life,
has made me incompetent to do anything else (which obviously isn't true), and has somehow kept me from reaching
maturity. I know, through Mephistopheles, that these reactions are connected with my mother, who was largely respon-
sible for my musical career. I shall go into this at length
farther on. Meanwhile let me describe the symptoms related
to work as they appeared during the breakdown and subsequent analysis.

The first great problem was to achieve sufficient stability to
be able to work and continue to earn my living. I had responsibilities, and psychoanalysis is expensive. Moreover,
when I am mentally disturbed, I nearly always feel a strong
necessity to get on, somehow, with the routine of life, as if

the mere repetition of familiar tasks is in itself reassuring. (By going through the motions of living, one can sometimes help convince oneself that one is actually living satisfactorily.) A rest somewhere away from my usual environment was out of the question for economic reasons. And I was afraid to go anywhere anyhow; I had to beat the demon on his own grounds. No use changing the scene. It would only complicate matters.

At first I was afraid to get out of bed. The extent of irrational terror that this involved is very difficult for anyone who has not been through a similar experience to understand. The leaden weight of one's arms; the lack of conviction that one can do so simple a thing as reach for a glass of water; the inability to concentrate on reading even a line or two of a book or newspaper; the terrific attacks of depression brought on by even the thought of undertaking any task or responsibility; the waves of terror that would rise and subside like spasms without any apparent cause at all; the physical manifestations —usually cramps in the intestinal tract or in the muscles of the legs and feet—all these things were daily and hourly experiences. In the beginning there was relief—very temporary relief—in two things: sleep (to which I would look forward every day, and got at night by means of barbiturates), and alcohol, which relaxed me slightly and enabled me to eat. The thought of suicide, which was continually present, also had an irrational motive. I desired death, not so much because of any particular resentment of, or disappointment with, life, but merely because it might deprive me of consciousness and thus relieve me of my symptoms. It is curious how a neurotic, in the middle of a catastrophic breakdown, will lose all awareness of the real reasons for his condition. There will seem to him to be only two protagonists in the battle he is fighting—himself and his irrational terror. He will treat this terror as a thing in itself, without looking into its causes, and attempt a grim game of avoiding, outwitting, and suppressing it. By great effort of the will, he can sometimes conquer it temporarily. But being ignorant of its causes, or even unwilling to discover its causes, he cannot get rid of it completely. His efforts will lead him into superstitious actions. He will convince himself that by counting up to a certain number (and bearing his terror up to this point) he can renew his strength. He will try to put faith in certain objects—a vase, a chair, a bedside clock—as if they had some magic qualities, and tell himself that as long as they are there, he will be all right.

The terror itself is, I am convinced, one of the most intolerable varieties of suffering a human being can experience. But what contributes most to this intolerability is the fact that one does not understand why the terror is there, and hence has no way of combating it. The popular remedies ("Get your mind on something else," "Stop worrying about yourself," "Feel blue? Just snap out of it.") don't work at all in the catastrophic state in which I found myself. I tried them repeatedly. In this plight, one attempts to shrug the whole mental state off as childish and irrational (which, in a way, it is— but the trouble is that one has not discovered precisely *why* it is irrational, and *in what* the contrary rationality would consist). One notes that physical and mental states interchange in a curious way: When one conquers one's mental depression sufficiently to stop thinking of suicide, one suddenly develops spasms in one's stomach; when these spasms finally subside so that one can eat, one experiences a return of all the mental depression. This mechanism turns out, in the circumstances, to be a great discovery. When the mental depression becomes intolerable, one can, almost at will, exchange it for an excruciating case of stomach cramps, and contrariwise, when one can bear the pain in one's stomach no longer, one can switch back to mental terror again. One soon gets tired of this game, however, since it leads only back and forth to different ends of the same cage. The fact remains that one is suffering intolerably, that one can see no way out of one's predicament, that one seems faced with either helpless invalidism or suicide. One is still afraid to get out of bed.

During this state I made two experiments. Writing has always been, for me, a method of mental discipline—a means of getting my mind off personal troubles by concentrating on a specific subject or idea. I had told my editor at *The New Yorker* that I would try to write another column. By a pure effort of the will, I tried writing in bed. I would steel myself to inventing a single sentence, grasp my pencil tightly, and force myself to put it down on paper. Then I could think up another sentence. The effort required was almost beyond my strength. After each sentence I would fall back into a state of acute anxiety which I would then attempt to conquer sufficiently to make the next try. I succeeded in turning out a paragraph. Later, when I read it, I discovered to my surprise that it was a very well-written, logical paragraph. But I got no farther. My anxiety became unbearable, and I relapsed into staring at the ceiling again. My second experiment was with reading, which had always been, for me, a pleasant form of escape and mental stimulation. I tried to read a detective story. But its preoccupation with violence and sex horrified me. I was continuously afraid that I would come across a scene that would somehow completely unhinge my mind. This form of escape was no longer possible. I tried reading philosophy, but was unable to concentrate on a single abstract idea. I think I must have felt that I had already tried philosophy and that obviously it had failed me as a remedy. I tried reading the Bible, but the results were the same. Finally I hit on something I could read, slowly and painfully, just as a method of passing the time. It was the Encyclopedia Britannica. I would turn the pages listlessly, reading whatever happened to be before me—biographies, descriptions of geographical regions, articles on forms of organic life, and so on. I do not know exactly why this type of reading succeeded where others failed. Perhaps it was because what I read was completely lacking in form. One could go on and on like a person involved in an endless job of knitting. The encyclopedia seemed quite unrelated to the problems of life, and, at the same time, it didn't threaten to create an illusion of any sort. It was simply a matter of words piled on words, or descriptions piled on descriptions, with a lack of cohesion similar to what one would find in a view from a train window.

But I couldn't go on as a madman sitting in solitude reading page after page of the encyclopedia. I knew that somehow I had to get out of bed and prepare to face my problems again. It was at this point that I realized that my own resources were not enough, and that if I were ever to escape from my predicament I must do so with outside help. I have always been a very independent person, and never, to my knowledge, have I asked another human being for help in any important matter. I had, in fact, clung to this independence as a sort of guarantee of my ability to get along in the world. So far, I had been able to depend on myself. But now, obviously, things had changed. I had read enough popular psychoanalytical literature to realize that I was in the grip of a severely exacerbated neurosis. I seemed powerless to combat it by myself, so I called up the psychiatrist. I did this with a certain feeling of foreboding. To me, it was a last resort—a sort of substitute for suicide, in which I was about to take leave of my life, or my personality, and see whether another could be built again from the ground up. It seemed that the step involved killing my present unsatisfactory self, and hoping that I could change into another person, freed of my present difficulties. I knew that many people had performed the operation successfully. After all, I had little or nothing to lose.

I had first met Mephistopheles at a cocktail party several years before, and I remember that, hearing that he was a psychiatrist, I deliberately set out to irritate him by praising the virtues of Catholic Thomist theology, with which I was well acquainted and which I knew to be at odds with the Freudian concept of life. This game was made even more exciting to me by the obvious fact that Mephistopheles was a Jew, and hence probably unsympathetic to Catholicism. The fact that I, myself, was no Catholic and believed very little of the doctrine I was upholding, seemed to me unimportant. I was trying to jolt a Jewish psychiatrist into a realization that his own smug way of looking at the world was not the only one. To my surprise, Mephistopheles didn't become irritated at all. He didn't seem a bit interested in arguing the point. He was entirely sympathetic. He was not interested in airing any beliefs of his own, or in countering what I pretended were mine. From subsequent acquaintance I know that he was merely acting like a psychiatrist. He wasn't interested so much in the views I was propounding as in the emotional reasons why I was propounding them. I became excited over my own eloquence and had a large number of cocktails. I don't know whether Mephistopheles said to himself, "This is obviously a very mixed-up fellow in a high state of tension. Sooner or later he is going to crack up and yell for my services." But he may have. At any rate, some three years later I remembered the meeting, and telephoned him. This time I was in no mood to try foisting some system of dialectics on an unwilling victim just for the fun of it.

He made an appointment with me. There were no preliminary hesitations on my part once I had taken the step. (The step itself had its difficulties for me, chief among which was the public admission that I was not normal mentally and could not get along without professional help. This seemed tantamount to admitting that I was not entirely sane, and once having made this admission I had no idea where it was going to lead—to an institution? to shock therapy?—at least to the placing of my mental faculties in the hands of a comparative stranger.) But there was the problem of transporting my physical body in a taxi some thirty city blocks to his office. This I attacked with great trepidation. I was determined to go by myself. Shaking with apprehension, I got out of bed and dressed for the first time in many weeks. I managed to navigate the stairs, got myself onto the sidewalk, and became nearly paralyzed with fear that I would be unable to find a taxi and would miss the appointment. There were other fears —that I would not succeed in getting home again afterward, that the whole venture would prove hopeless, since I was already rather old to undertake psychiatric treatment. I finally managed to stop a taxi, and got into it.

My first surprise was that Mephistopheles had his office not in one of those elegant Park Avenue suites that psychiatrists occupy in the movies, but in a rather old, rambling apartment where he lived with his family. His waiting room was comparatively dark, which I found comforting, and it was decorated with an incredible variety of paintings, statuary, archaeological relics, and other knickknacks. This variety was so great that it could not possibly have reflected the personal taste of one individual—so I guessed that the whole array was an accretion of gifts from grateful patients, and that probably Mephistopheles had to keep them all on permanent display for fear of hurting somebody's feelings. I soon learned the ritual of entering the door to Mephistopheles' apartment. It was always open. One simply rang to announce one's presence, entered without further ceremony, and sat in the waiting room until called. The same openness and availability seemed to apply to reaching Mephistopheles by telephone. He would always answer in person, and would even interrupt the most crucial psychiatric session to talk to some other patient who had a problem to discuss.

My second surprise was that there was no trick overhead lighting in Mephistopheles' office, that I didn't lie on a couch, that I was not subjected to a Rorschach test, that no list of words was read for the purpose of dragging associations out of my subconscious. I simply sat in a chair opposite his desk and talked. I was so amazed by the absence of theatrical props and complex methods that I asked Mephistopheles, somewhere around the third session, whether I was, in fact, being psychoanalyzed. He assured me that I was. Apparently psychoanalytical techniques had changed considerably since I had read about them in books by Freud and Jung. Actually it was simply a conversation in which I did nearly all the talking.

It was several months (mostly at a rate of five sessions a week) before my symptoms showed any real tendency to disappear. During this period I talked continuously at the sessions, amazed at the quantity of mere verbiage I brought up. I wanted to get over my symptoms; I wanted to be a good patient (i.e., to hold back nothing and to make a complete confession of all my impulses and feelings). I was a little self-

conscious in the very zeal with which I attacked the problem.
I had a certain amount of superficial knowledge about psychoanalysis, and I invented interpretations and diagnoses of my
own, nearly all of which proved to be inaccurate or erroneous.
Because of my difficulties with women, I was afraid that perhaps I was a frustrated homosexual, and that psychoanalysis
would reveal this. However, I faced this fear squarely and
brought out a mass of anecdotes concerning what seemed to
me practically insane sexual behavior. Mephistopheles was
offering me no advice and making no decisions whatever for
me. When I asked what I should do, he merely shrugged his
shoulders, accused me of asking for magic formulas, and told
me that it was entirely up to me. His job, apparently, was
simply to listen, and then to point out certain inconsistencies
in my rationalizations of my behavior. He interpreted any
question like, "What shall I do?" not as something demanding
an answer, but simply as a cry of fear. He pointed out to me
the obvious fact that I was terrified, and kept asking what it
was that I was afraid of. I tried to answer this question repeatedly. I even invented fears that I didn't really feel. I
dragged up all sorts of fears from my childhood that I had
long ceased to feel: fears of insects, of violence, of ghost
stories, of the dark, and so on.

Meanwhile the grip of fear continued, though the idea that
I might someday be cured kept me going. I had by this time
lost a great deal of weight. I was very thin and pale, and became additionally depressed every time I looked in a mirror.
It seemed necessary to keep in motion—to have something to
do. I couldn't, at first, bear to go near my office, so I began
taking long walks about the city. It is hard for me today to
recall the exact state of mind I had during these walks. I know
by the altered speed with which I approached successive

changing traffic lights that I was walking very slowly, perhaps at less than half my customary stride. I must have been shuffling along like an old man. I remember that it seemed to give me a little feeling of added confidence that I could put one foot before the other and continue this process almost indefinitely. I occasionally lifted my eyes and attempted to concentrate on, or fix my interest in, the things around me. Sometimes I would notice details of old New York architecture and decide vaguely that I preferred one kind of building to another. But most of the time my eyes were on the sidewalk in front of me, and my mind was occupied entirely with a numb struggle against terror. Since I hoped eventually to be cured, the mere passage of time seemed to take on significance. Every evening I was glad that I had managed to put another day behind me successfully. Curiously, time did seem to pass rather quickly.

As the analysis of fear progressed, I began to discover a few things about my particular terrors. There were a lot of them, and they were quite varied. In asking myself what I was afraid of, I had jumped to all sorts of conclusions. But little by little, I was able to discard the spurious fears and get a rough idea of the areas in which the real ones lay. I was afraid, apparently, of any contact with people, including my closest friends and my wife. I was afraid of any work that was done with a feeling of seriousness and hence involved a sense of responsibility. (Actual daily work at the office had, of course, become utterly impossible. I remained home on sick leave.) I was afraid of traps of any kind—afraid to get into a bus for fear I wouldn't be able to get out at any moment I desired; afraid to engage anybody in conversation, lest I shouldn't be able to terminate it and walk away if I felt the impulse; afraid to venture far from my home lest something prevent me from returning. On the physical plane I was afraid of my stomach cramps, my continual feeling of giddiness and weakness, and so on. I was also paralyzed with fear at my own sexual urges, which I had no way of gratifying normally (relations with my wife had long since ceased) and which became a channel through which all my anxieties expressed themselves. Anxiety would inevitably produce a strong sexual urge. But the gratification of this urge demanded contact with people (women), and I was afraid of people. This dilemma led to autoeroticism, followed by intolerable feelings of guilt, isolation, and self-condemnation. It was hard to tell which was the more horrible, the almost unbearable anxiety preceding autoerotic acts or the self-condemnatory depression that followed them.

I discussed all these things repeatedly with Mephistopheles, and soon became aware of an important distinction between types of fear. On one hand there were symptoms of my malady: fears of people, traps, work, and so on. On the other hand there was another enormous fear which was a fear of fear itself—a sort of helpless panic brought on by the terror of being subjected to the symptoms. This latter fear I was able gradually to bring under control and separate from the symptoms. I could isolate the symptoms—fear of people, of traps, of work—know how they would make me react, and prepare to bear the pain of my reactions. And the fear of fear itself could be controlled by simply talking myself out of it and realizing that it was of all my fears the most irrational. This was an important step, though a very difficult one to take. What it amounted to was a declaration that I was not entirely helpless. I was the victim of a severe neurosis, but I had begun to define the neurosis and to abolish the fear that coping with it was entirely beyond my powers. It was a little like fighting a battle after having discovered where the enemy was, and gaining a few vague ideas about his strength and weapons.

Mephistopheles had mentioned another fear which he called a fear of self-assertion, but it was months before I was able to see what he meant by this term. I made several vague attempts to understand him. How should I set about asserting myself? I tried being deliberately impolite to people. One evening, I even took to bumping into people on the street without apologizing. But this didn't seem to help. Obviously the field in which I had failed to assert myself lay somewhere else. It was only later that I discovered that this field really lay in the area surrounding my responsibilities—my traps, my work, and the people on whom I had the greatest dependence—mainly my wife.

The main objective at the outset was to continue earning my living. My employers at the office were very kind and understanding. They agreed not to burden me with any very taxing work for the time being, but I knew that this semi-invalid status could not last forever. I had to regain my ability to write. Mephistopheles, in one of his rare admonitory statements, had advised me not to consider any responsibility as a matter of life or death. He had also introduced a concept entirely new to me, which was to regard life as a gamble. I had always demanded certainties—both of the world and myself. If I said I would do a certain thing at a certain time, I was the kind of fellow who performed exactly according to specifications, even if I killed myself in the process. I had accepted all responsibilities in this spirit. Failure of any sort had, to me, been a disgrace. And at this point, I was, of course, deep in the most spectacular failure of my life. The gambler's approach had always been foreign to me. I had even disliked sports and games because of the element of uncertainty that I would win. But now, I began to realize that there are no certainties, that life is, in fact, a gamble, and that one is not obliged to win every time. This, first of all, applied to my writing. It had, in the past, been inconceivable to me that I could write a bad piece, and the necessity of always writing a good one had put an intolerable burden on me. As I look back on it, I now realize that I had been in the habit of approaching each job of writing in more or less of a panic, then mastering my panic by main force, and driving myself through in a great state of excitement. It had been quite customary for me to develop a violent fit of indigestion and several nights of insomnia every time I wrote an article. On certain occasions (once in the middle of India), I forced myself to write articles in a real state of outward as well as inward panic, and became almost unable to eat or sleep at all. This sort of thing usually happened most violently when I was working against a deadline and dared not fail. Now, it seems rather elementary and silly to lay such stress on this point, but when Mephistopheles suggested that it wouldn't be a matter of life or death if I failed to make a deadline or if I wrote an inferior article, I realized that I had never considered my work from this point of view. This was, to me, a whole new concept: One went through life *trying*. One tried to write an article. One tried to write it well. One tried to get it done by a certain time. It was quite possible that one would fail at all these things. But, suppose one did? Well, that wouldn't mean death and destruction. That would merely mean that one had failed that time, and could start trying again. One relied to a certain extent on chance, and hence, one was spared the intolerable responsibility of being absolutely certain of one's results. This principle—of treating work as a gamble—also spread to other aspects of life. One tried to eat, for example, or one tried to spend an evening talking to people, or one tried to go to the office. If one failed, and ended in a state of panic, one simply wrote it off as a bad try and then tried again. There was considerable emotional relief to be found in this attitude. The relief lay in dropping part of the burden of responsibility and letting fate carry it. This notion, I am aware, is one that comes to nearly everybody who undertakes psychoanalysis at one time or another, but to me it was quite new.

I must have presented a somewhat curious spectacle to my colleagues when I finally put in an appearance at my office. My first expedition there, and my first attempts to cope with the simplest sort of work, were handled on the above-described trial-and-error principle. The idea of even entering the elevator in the building was terrifying. The presence of other people—even though I knew most of them well—was also terrifying. Fortunately, a number of my colleagues, who knew all about my breakdown, handled the situation with great tact. They never forced the slightest responsibility on me; they tried to interest me in little jobs in which I advised them on matters of taste while they did all the real work; they deferred to me in every way, and repeatedly made a point of assuring me of their high regard. I couldn't have been more gently handled if they had been trained wardens in an institution. Somebody in authority, I think—probably Ed Thompson, who was then managing editor—must have passed the word around, and an organized policy was in force that I was to be treated like a piece of breakable china. I noted the prevailing kindness around me, and was very grateful. It showed that my illness was being taken very seriously; it also showed that the organization I worked for considered me valuable enough to spend some time and effort helping me salvage myself. Later on I was to learn that an extraordinary number of my colleagues had undergone psychotherapy at one time or another, and that many of them understood my plight as well as, or better than, I did.

But while this kind treatment alleviated my troubles greatly, I still had my own fighting to do. I returned to the office, as I have explained, on a trial-and-error basis. That is, I tried to walk across town to the office, conscious all the time that I was perfectly free to turn around and walk home again. I succeeded in reaching the office, then tried coping with the elevator (which was much more frightening, since I could not get out at will and my motion from place to place was in control of another person, the elevator boy). I was scared, but again I succeeded. Then I tried to go into my office and sit at my desk. Here I was using a psychological mechanism I have noted before in connection with walking and so on—the mechanism of "going through the motions." I was quite aware that I would not be able to do any work. But if I could succeed in sitting at my desk (i.e., in taking the physical position associated with working, and giving the outward appearance of a man at work) I felt that I might somehow gain renewed confidence. Here, however, I failed completely. I was able to force myself to enter my office, but the moment I sat at my desk I was overcome with unbearable panic and had to get up again. As long as I was standing on my feet I seemed prepared either to fight or to flee. But the minute I sat down I seemed caught in an inescapable trap. This failure to be able to sit at my desk was not only discouraging in itself; it also brought on a recurrence of the awful fear of fear. Since I was unable to do so simple and natural a thing, I became reconvinced of my own hopeless irrationality, and frightened all over again at my general plight. The fear of the symptoms had reasserted itself. I spent a few minutes walking up and down the hallways trying to collect myself, and then got into the elevator in a great state of trepidation, reached the ground floor, and shakily made my way home to bed again.

In a situation like this one feels bound, at any cost, to form habits. Once one has learned to do something over and over again in spite of one's fear, one gains confidence merely from the fact that one has repeatedly accomplished the task, however difficult it may have seemed. I had not succeeded in sitting at my desk, but I had succeeded in getting to my office and getting back again. I resolved to go to my office every day. This was a motion I had already accomplished, and failure to continue it would have meant falling back from the little progress I had made. So I returned to my office next day, and every working day from then on, going through a grim ritual that proved little by little that I could give the outward appearance of a man who was doing something to earn his living. I managed to cope with another terrifying problem. I had to eat lunch, and this demanded that I sit in a restaurant long enough to get some food into my stomach. Sitting at a restaurant table was nearly as difficult as sitting at my desk. But here more fundamental problems were involved. One had to eat, otherwise one would starve. Obviously then, one had to sit at a restaurant table whether one liked it or not. Eating with other people was out of the question. I was afraid of people. I ate alone, always in a state of panic which I suppressed outwardly and which often caused the sweat to run down my face from the effort I was making. I don't think I would have been successful except for my habit of taking two or three drinks of whiskey before each meal. I had still not solved the problem of being able to sit at my desk. At the office I remained on my feet, pacing the hallways, occasionally attempting a conversation or looking on and commenting a little while my colleagues worked.

II

It is obvious to me, as I write this, that this peculiar inability to sit at my desk must have reflected a deep resentment over something connected with my work. The resentment was not directed exclusively at the work itself, for I now had little or no difficulty in remaining seated at the desk in my room at home, where I had often written both articles for *Life* magazine and work of my own. Several months later I was given, temporarily, a large, dignified office in a better and quieter location, and found that I could sit at the desk in that office with reasonable calmness. On being moved back to my original office after a few weeks, however, I had a recurrence of unwillingness to sit at the desk. In the course of months of effort I conquered the phobia sufficiently to sit there without experiencing panic. But even now, after a year and a half of therapy, I am still unwilling to sit there. I have not, during this time, done any important writing at that desk. And today, after sitting there for a few minutes, I invariably find myself getting up and pacing the hallways. There is obviously something about sitting at that desk that I find profoundly distasteful and disturbing. What? A dislike of work? But I do not dislike my work, and I have now learned to do it well enough elsewhere—at home, for example. A feeling that I am being humiliated by being expected to sit there? This is probably closer to the truth. There was, in fact, a deep-rooted association with that desk (which was just like the desk in the office of any other *Time-Life* writer) that seemed to say, "If you sit here you are just an ordinary hack journalist, without honor, a cog in a machine, without individuality. You cannot sit there and maintain any illusion of independence or dignity." This interpretation of the phobia is further confirmed by the fact that I had no difficulty sitting at the desk of the other, quieter and more dignified office that I occupied for a couple of months. (I suspect that my editors had put me there as a therapeutic measure.) In the beginning, when the feeling had the proportions of a true phobia, it was intensified by the notion that the desk was a trap, and that if I remained seated at it, I would not be able to get away from it at will.

During my first attempts to cope with the desk phobia I tried my hand as a picture editor, thinking that perhaps this sort of work would prove less taxing than writing. I found myself sitting in an advisory capacity with an art editor and a photographer, arranging an elaborate pictorial layout concerned with the sculpture of ancient India. I found that, provided nobody made demands that I stay any stipulated amount of time or that I get any stipulated amount of work done, I could participate for a considerable stretch—say an hour or two—in these layout sessions. It is true that I did not sit down during the sessions. I remained standing and poised, as it were, for instant flight, if that proved necessary. My colleagues seemed to understand, and made allowances for my difficulties. I usually excused myself when the impulse to leave became too strong to bear, and often this impulse would reach the breaking point in the middle of an important discussion, leaving a decision hanging in the air. But I left when I felt like it, and my colleagues made no move to stop me. Little by little I was able to remain longer at these sessions, and though I actually contributed nothing much of value, the relative success of the experiment was somewhat encouraging.

My first attempts to resume my career as a writer were more difficult, for here I was approaching a crucial problem. Making picture layouts was not my *métier,* and there was no great stake involved; if I failed to make a good layout I could always excuse my failure by saying, "After all, nobody expects me to be a layout editor—my real job is writing." With writing there was no such excuse possible. People expected me to write well, and I expected good writing of myself. This was a field where failure had been intolerable, and where the responsibility for success had been a burden I had carried with pride and considerable attendant anxiety. Writing was my method of earning a living, and to fail at it meant economic catastrophe as well as wounded pride. The breakdown had, as I have already explained, left me utterly unable to write. It was necessary, first, to study and analyze the nature of my fear of writing, and, second, to find some practical method of coping with this fear. In overcoming these problems, Mephistopheles was very helpful. The outward symptoms were plain: Every time I grasped a pencil and attempted to put a single word of professional magazine writing on paper, I was suddenly overcome with panic. I could suppress this panic for very short periods and force myself, by a grim effort of the will, to write a sentence or two, but I would then develop attacks of depression, indigestion, and intestinal spasms, violent autoerotic impulses, cramps in the muscles of the legs and feet, and so on. Ultimately I would have to take to my bed, where I would lie in an acute state of anxiety, trying desperately to allay my fears and collect myself. Curiously, however, I soon discovered that I could do other types of writing—rather aimless attempts at fiction, for example—without rousing any such violent fears. My fears, therefore, were not due to the mere act of writing, but to something connected with the specific job of writing magazine articles for publication. Here there was responsibility. The writing had to be up to certain standards. I dared not fail, and I was in fact failing to write, precisely because of my fear of failure. What was apparently a fear of writing was not actually that at all: It was a fear of failing to meet specifications of quality imposed on me by my editors, and, more significantly, by myself. I seemed incapable of writing a word when I felt that this word was going to be judged by others, and when my livelihood depended on its meeting certain competitive standards. As in my relations with people, I had lost all confidence in my ability to compete, and had become unwilling to take the slightest action which placed me in a vulnerable position (vulnerable, in this case, meaning subject to criticism by others). Seen from any reasonably normal point of view my predicament was a somewhat childish one. Apparently in my disturbed mind, I regarded my editors, my readers, and my competitors as tremendously powerful people who could annihilate me utterly if what I did met with their slightest disapproval. The cost of failure seemed so overwhelming that I was simply unwilling to make the smallest attempt at success.

Having clarified the nature of this fear through repeated conversations with Mephistopheles, I began, as I had in facing other problems, by submitting to the trial-and-error method. First, I had to accept the idea that success was not guaranteed —trial after trial might end in failure, and this failure was not necessarily an overwhelming disgrace. As with going to the office, meeting people, and sitting at my desk, failure could be written off as a bad try, and one could try again. Writing was not very different from other functions of life. One could not depend on certainties; one could only try and hope. Second, I had to abolish, by some means, the inordinate sense of pressure connected with my work. This pressure seemed to come from two sources—the "deadline" (viz., the notion that I must have a certain amount of work finished by a certain time), and the need for perfection (viz., the feeling that every sentence, every paragraph, and every article must be perfect, and that the penalty for imperfection was some vaguely sensed and utterly horrible catastrophe). Both these sources of pressure were quite irrational and imaginary. My editors, aware of my condition, had put no pressure of any kind on me. I had no deadlines to meet, and nobody seemed to expect me to produce anything. As to perfection, I was quite aware that during my career as a journalist I had turned out a considerable amount of imperfect writing. Actually, perfection was not expected of me. Nevertheless, the fact that I was drawing a weekly salary even during my illness, put me under a sense of obligation. I must, in time, succeed in earning that salary, and in order to do so, I must be able to meet deadlines and write again with reasonable assurance. In the near future, somehow I must manage to achieve success in this objective.

My first attempt to write an article involved several complex factors. I deliberately decided that I would write on a musical subject, because, knowing a great deal about music, I could depend on my own knowledge to a certain extent and

avoid the social problems entailed in interviewing and the
extra effort involved in observation and research. Since I was
a practical journalist, however, I could not avoid these problems entirely. My article had to have something to do with
contemporary news. The opportunity came when Gian-Carlo
Menotti, one of the few composers I admired, produced his
opera *The Consul* for the first time on Broadway. I decided
to try an article on Menotti, with the usual biographical material included in a *Life* "close-up," as it was called, but
leaning heavily on the criticism and evaluation of his work,
which I was already well acquainted with. I was too terrified
of people to consider the idea of interviewing Menotti personally. I thought I might get over this hurdle by sending an
assistant to talk to him. After all, I had met Menotti, knew
many of his acquaintances, and had already formed some
conception of his character. Thus, I got around all the social
problems except one—I had to go to hear the performance of
The Consul. Ever since I had cracked up on my outside job
as music critic for *The New Yorker*, I had been as scared to
sit through a musical performance in an auditorium as I had
been to sit at my office desk. I did manage to sit through *The
Consul*, however. I accomplished this feat by drinking a good
deal of whiskey beforehand, and by assuring myself that I
was only trying: I might fail to be able to sit there, and consequently have to abandon the idea of doing the article. "Well,
what of it?" I told myself. "If that happens, I shall simply drop
the idea, and do my first article on something else." The
change of attitude worked. I not only managed to sit through
the opera; I even enjoyed parts of it.

After sending my assistant to gather certain biographical
and personal details in an interview with Menotti himself,
I embarked on writing the piece. I started fully prepared for

some difficult emotional development. Sure enough, the first day I failed to get a word on paper, and after a desperate struggle with panic I took to my bed again. The second day I tried again. This time I had taken a more modest approach. I dropped the whole idea of getting the article done in the foreseeable future. In fact, I took the attitude that it didn't matter a bit whether I got it done at all. I even managed to convince myself that I was not seriously occupied in writing an article—that I was just scribbling at random on something that might conceivably turn out to be part of an article but that would probably be thrown away. What I was doing, of course, was absolving myself in advance for any responsibility for the quality of my product. In this state of mind I managed to write, fairly fluently and without overwhelming anxiety, about six hundred words. I never even brought a critical eye to bear on them when I had finished. I simply laid them aside and lay down to rest. Next day I added another six or seven hundred words. After about five days' desultory work of this sort I read over what I had written, discovered that it was not too bad for publication, and felt considerably encouraged. In a little over a week I put a fairly good finish on the piece, took it to my editors, and was glad to find that they wanted to publish it. I had learned that given certain circumstances and a certain attitude of mind, it was possible for me to continue writing articles. This was an important step, for I had not touched a pencil to paper or used a typewriter for six months.

But my troubles with writing were by no means over. I have described the circumstances of writing this particular article in considerable detail. I am not going into similar detail on subsequent ones. They all involved the same problems. The start of several later ones left me paralyzed with fear and seeking my bed again, trembling and grasping desperately for control of my panic. But in the end the method always worked: to pretend that I was not seriously concerned with what I was writing, that it didn't matter when it was finished, or whether it was finished at all; above all to abolish all sense of hurry and all feeling that I was obliged to please my editors or even myself. A few months later I even managed my first interview, with a movie actress. Fortunately, she and I both drank a good deal and she apparently found my extreme shyness and illness-at-ease rather engaging. I was not able to perform the interview with my onetime expertness. I had ceased to be able to drive myself as a good interviewer must, keeping an indelible record of conversation and observation in the mind while thinking up a continuous stream of leading questions (a fatiguing job even for a normally functioning mind). Again I left most of the detailed questioning to my assistant. Nevertheless I managed the human contact necessary for an interview—and that was another step forward. I had not yet learned to enjoy the process of writing again, or to approach it with genuine enthusiasm. But I was learning to function sufficiently well to earn my living.

The extra job writing for *The New Yorker*, it now appeared, had involved another factor. I was back writing about music, dealing again with an art that was associated in my mind with personal failure and with my mother. (I had already served as a music critic on the dailies before I went to work for *Time* and *Life*, and I had regarded my work as a general journalist for *Life* in the light of an emancipation from everything connected with music.) Still another factor had been the rather exaggerated respect in which I held *The New Yorker*. I had always written for *Life* magazine with a slight feeling of condescension. It was, after all, a large, rather vulgar mass-circulation magazine whose intellectual standards were not too high. I felt that I could write for it with one hand tied behind my back, and this feeling that I was potentially able to do a far better job than *Life* actually demanded made me quite confident of my ability to write for it. But *The New Yorker* was a different proposition, or so I felt at the time. *The New Yorker* was held in high esteem by people whose taste I respected. My writing for it must therefore be exemplary; if I failed to achieve perfection here I could not excuse myself by saying that I was just turning out stuff to amuse the masses. I felt that *The New Yorker* demanded my best efforts, and my attempt to achieve perfection under the continuous pressure entailed in holding down the two jobs produced a burden that ultimately proved intolerable. Now, looking back, I can see that my enormous reverence for the prestige of *The New Yorker* was somewhat naïve. It is, after all, just a magazine, though it is one with very high standards. But at the time, the honor of writing for it seemed overwhelming—and this honor conferred upon me the attendant obligation of being the most skillful writer on music in the world. As a matter of fact the music criticism I wrote for *The New Yorker* was exceedingly good. But the consciousness that it must be exceedingly good week after week caused no end of panic, and ultimately contributed to complete collapse. It was from this perfectionist attitude, with its ending in breakdown, that I was gradually recovering. I was now approaching my writing from the opposite point of view—with deliberate carelessness and studied avoidance of responsibility.

This point of view was obviously a temporary expedient necessitated by my mentally disturbed state. It was, at the time, desirable above all to prove that I could practice my craft successfully even on the most inefficient and imperfect basis. I dare say that I can someday cope again with a desire for finer quality, and begin to take pride in my work. As I write this, however, I am conscious that I have not yet achieved this degree of confidence. I have, however, achieved an ability to tolerate my symptoms which I had never before dreamed possible. I now find that by not seeking to avoid extreme depression—by allowing it to take its course, by even wallowing in it—being utterly miserable and showing outward symptoms of misery—I can find new strength. In this way I am able to prove that I can withstand the most distressing forms of depression.

I have explained earlier the importance of certain discoveries I made in the first few months of analysis: the discovery that the fear of the symptoms could be dissociated from the symptoms themselves (which entailed the possibility of rejecting the feeling of absolute helplessness); the subsequent discovery that though one could not depend on certainties, one could try and hope, trying again if one failed temporarily; and, finally, the discovery that I could withstand the worst symptoms. To these was added another discovery—that depressed and anxious mental states are not entirely mysterious and unfathomable aberrations which one must fight to suppress or ignore, but that they arise from quite definite, though somewhat devious, causes. This discovery was also extremely important. It was the discovery that there was actually method in the madness. It gave me the tool with which I could study the symptoms instead of suppressing them. Anxiety is not, as it often seems, a horrifying supernatural source of martyrdom which must be borne with stoical desperation. Its symptoms are often quite irrational, but the causes of these symptoms are as definite, and as subject to rational study, as the causes of a broken leg or an infectious disease. This fact is, I sup-

pose, one of the great contributions made by Sigmund Freud
to the field of mental pathology. Neuroses are, in fact, diseases, and may be treated and cured as such. Because of the
complexity of the human mind, these diseases are very complex and their causes are very difficult to isolate. But psychoanalysis, or interview therapy, offers an admirable method of
digging them out. And once exposed to the light of day, they
can be seen for what they are, and measures can be taken to
cope with them. The mere statement of this fact may seem a
commonplace to anyone who has undergone psychoanalysis,
or even read anything about modern methods of psychotherapy. Actually, the general notion that mental aberration follows certain laws and is curable, is taken for granted by most
literate people today. Nevertheless there is a great difference
between accepting this notion as one of the numerous interesting facts of modern scientific advance, and actually applying its principles to the study of one's own psychic
disturbances. Here it seems to come as a fresh revelation. It
is easy to pity the insane and rejoice in the fact that methods
have been discovered for the alleviation of their plight. It is
altogether different to declare oneself insane, so to speak, and
then to apply the devious and complicated tools of psychotherapy to one's own mind. In the latter case one learns by
direct experience. One is in the position of a man who has
thrown himself into a torrent and comes painfully, but grate-
fully, to the realization that there are established and well-
reasoned methods by which he can keep himself afloat. In
time he ceases to flounder hopelessly and learns to apply his
mind to the technique of surviving. It may be years before he
swims with confidence and ease; but the principle is there—
and that fact alone is consoling.

The gradual discovery of these principles as they apply to

one's own behavior amounts, I suppose, to the gradual discovery of the true self. As I write this, I have not by any means penetrated any but the more obvious causes of my personal conflicts. I have, so far, been occupied mainly with the difficult problem of finding a *modus vivendi* which will keep me afloat while I pursue my studies of the deeper causes. But I can already discern certain firm outlines in the sea of irrationality that surrounds me. Most of these outlines, as might be expected, have come into view through a deeper understanding of lifelong habits and attitudes that have their origins in the obscure and long-forgotten events of childhood.

From the very start of analysis, certain vague impulses, desires, and fears began to manifest themselves in symbolic or mythological form—in dreams, fantasies, and irrational behavior. It is a curious thing how, when the lid of habitual suppression is gradually lifted, the unconscious mind behaves like some long-imprisoned animal and strives instinctively to cooperate in any effort that is being made toward its release. It is as if it were trying desperately to communicate with your consciousness and saying to you, "At last, I see, you have arrived at the sensible idea of freeing me after all these years. I can help you in this task if you will listen to what I have to say." What the unconscious mind says, under these circumstances, may approach a veritable flood of vague and fantastic ideas, all conveyed in symbols which demand expert interpretation to be understood. Often the interpretations, even in expert hands, are incorrect. But when they are correct, the unconscious immediately signals the message, "You were right that time!" It does so by ceasing its pressure for the moment and allowing you a temporary release from your anxiety.

These communications from the unconscious often took the form of eccentric behavior, phobias, liking for, or aversion to, certain objects or persons, waking fantasies, and impulses that were more or less veiled when talked about. The phobia about sitting at my office desk, for example, was such a communication—one whose precise meaning I have not yet, at this writing, discovered, though it undoubtedly concerns a strong unconscious resentment toward the circumstances in which I work. But often the clearest and most pertinent communications took the form of dreams which I remembered and recounted, as is customary, during analytical sessions. I discovered early that a great many of my dreams were as enigmatic to Mephistopheles as they were to me, and that the interpretation of many others was to a great extent a matter of guesswork. Still, taken in conjunction with the material brought up in the interviews, they often had obvious pertinence to dominant problems, and served to throw light on how I really felt as opposed to how I consciously thought I felt. Among the most useful ones were those dealing with Mephistopheles himself, and these he always studied eagerly in order to gauge my current mental attitude toward him and toward therapy. Some of these were hostile, involving attacks on some facet of Mephistopheles' personality. I would dream that a Jew had given me a pair of shoes to wear, that they didn't fit and were filthy inside. I would wake up exclaiming: "That damned Jew!" (Mephistopheles was a Jew.) Or I would dream that I was on a fantastic theatrical stage taking part in an operatic production, and that the music was of poor quality because it was composed of cheap Balkan and Hungarian tunes (Mephistopheles was a Hungarian); or I would dream that a Negro had stolen my wallet (Mephistopheles was charging me high fees). Some of the dreams represented a more cooperative attitude, where Mephistopheles would appear disguised as a guide who was assisting me through a cavern or some other menacing region, or as the conductor of a train in which I was riding, or as my father. Sometimes I would feel rejected by Mephistopheles and the dreams might depict me as an unwelcome visitor at a party in his house, where he would ignore me and devote his attention to his family and guests. Occasionally the phenomenon called "transference" would be complete even in a sexual sense. This is a curious manifestation. I had never understood how a male patient, unless he was a homosexual, could reach the state of "being in love with" a male analyst. And it is true that, on the conscious level, numerous taboos would interfere with such a development. In the dream world, however, the signs would sometimes be unmistakable. I would have very satisfying erotic or semierotic dreams involving such things as a beautiful woman who had hair of the same reddish color as Mephistopheles', or wore buttons similar to those on his coat, or where I played a game with numerals which, on awakening, I found to be the number of his street address. These dreams, expressing love, hatred, suspicion of, or confidence in, Mephistopheles became very frequent during the analysis, and often threw important light on the success, or lack of it, with which I was submitting to the therapy. Often, of course, the dreams were in direct contradiction to my conscious attitudes, in which case the dreams were usually presumed to contain the correct answer.

There were also numerous recurrent dreams, or rather casts of characters, scenery, and props which would manifest themselves over and over again. Among them I remember certain archetypes and certain locales usually connected with emotional states. There were dreams, for example, of imminent danger in which animals, particularly dogs, would appear. I would recurrently find myself making my way through heavy traffic at an intersection, meanwhile trying to keep a dog that accompanied me from being run over. The connotation of traffic and danger dated from early childhood, when, like most city-bred youngsters, I was warned repeatedly about crossing the street. The feeling of love and responsibility toward dogs and other animals was also deeply ingrained in me in childhood, and was the source of several violent conflicts which I shall explain later in another place. These dreams of danger usually occurred at times when I felt myself critically threatened by some situation in real life. The dog who was being protected was unquestionably myself.

Another category of recurrent dreams was that of having failed in some way to meet a situation which I felt to be crucial. Sometimes these dreams were about simple failures to arrive at an appointment on time. Often it was a boat or a train that I was desperately trying to board, but which left without me. The popular expression "to miss the boat," with all its possible metaphorical connotations, was implied in these dreams. Often I would find myself trying to get somewhere in a hurry and being foiled at every step by traffic, mechanical breakdowns, and other frustrations. Frequently these dreams took on a more specific character related to my career. Apparently my acceptance, at about the age of twenty-two, of failure in my childhood ambition to become a symphony conductor, still rankles on the unconscious level. In a very common recurrent dream I am about to step before an audience and conduct a symphony concert. But I am invariably frustrated. Either I find that I have arrived too late and the concert is over, or I find myself unable to reach the stage because people or objects are in the way, or I start to conduct, but find that only one or two musicians have arrived and the concert is out of the question, and so on.

Among the recurrent locales in my dreams is an unbelievably beautiful countryside which always resembles the landscape around a suburb of San Francisco where I spent the comparatively protected years of adolescence with my father and mother. Another such locale is a rather sinister, dirty-looking, and badly lit swimming pool deep in the basement of a building, and suffused with an atmosphere of damp, subterranean confinement. This I have not identified. Still another is what might be called "the tight place." It is a narrow passage which I reach after making my way through a cave or other confined pathway. It is so narrow that I cannot squeeze through, though I can see a "promised land" on the other side.

Dreams entailing self-condemnation, with me, sometimes take a humorous turn in which I am dressed in ridiculous clothes or am clowning in some undignified manner (sometimes deliberately playing a musical instrument raucously or out of tune). More often they are concerned with toilets and defecation. I am going to the toilet but can find no privacy and am forced to manage things in public, and with a feeling of humiliation. Or I want to go to the toilet and find that the only available one is incredibly filthy. Toilet paper is wet, dirty, and unusable. Sometimes, with a feeling of horror, I even find myself falling into the toilet bowl. The identification of guilt with defecation is, of course, one of the most prevalent of infantile associations, and this sort of dream has frequently occurred with me in an emotional situation where a feeling of guilt is pronounced.

There is, of course, a certain futility about trying to list types of dreams as I have just been doing. This is because the realistic description of the dream often fails to convey its true content, which is often expressed in a wholly personal system of symbolism, and can only be arrived at by free association and painstaking analysis during the waking state. No two people, in all probability, have the same vocabulary of dream symbols—the same mythological cast of characters. Each individual has his own. And it is, of course, true that a large number of dreams resist this sort of analysis and remain completely enigmatic.

There is one category, however, that is fairly definite and very important, and which I have so far neglected to mention except in a passing reference to dreams about the psychoanalyst. This is the category of the erotic dream. I have, like most people, I imagine, had erotic dreams ever since earliest childhood, and their peculiar symbolism, developed long before I had any conscious knowledge of the nature of sex, still persists to a certain extent in dreams of this sort today. Only since the age of twenty, when I had gained some actual experience of sex, have these dreams entailed the sexual act itself. And even now the majority of them depict a peculiar sort of personal mythology in which the act of intercourse is symbolized by fetishes and objects that have, actually, no relation to it. The paraphernalia of this dream mythology, based on childhood fantasies, even extends into my waking life, where it imposes itself upon my practical relations with women, often rendering them extremely unsatisfactory or difficult. Somewhere back in the mysterious alleyways of childish imagining, I must have sensed the power of the sexual urge, identified the object as female, and then attempted to explain it. Since I had no conception of the organic physical function, and undoubtedly suffered from extreme taboos regarding the nature of the male and female sex organs, I apparently created substitutes. The substitute where the female was concerned, in my case, was a woman's hair, which was longer than a man's, and thus seemed the most important distinguishing mark of the female as opposed to the male. Actually, in my childish imagination, a woman's long hair (these were the days before short hair became fashionable, and women wore their hair very long) became the symbol of the female sex organ, and became surrounded with a whole series of desires and taboos. I remember being extremely embarrassed as a child in the presence of women when they were combing their hair. This embarrassment was accompanied by a certain fascination, and by a stimulation of sexual urges. They seemed, in my childish imagination, to be exhibiting themselves to me sexually— something that aroused both desire and resentment, the latter because it threatened a violation of a taboo. Also the possession of long hair seemed to place women in a special and admired category among human beings. It was the badge of that group of beings with whom I desired contact. This brought about a peculiar emotional condition somewhat analagous to the penis envy that is so common in the psychological development of little girls. Long hair was something highly desirable, possessed only by women, and I envied them their possession of it. This envy set up a serious conflict, for, though I desired to possess long hair (i.e., a female sex organ) I was deeply anxious not to be considered feminine. Like most little boys, I considered it the last word in humiliation to be thought in any way to resemble a girl. The conflict was considerably intensified, I think, by the fact that my mother was a very dominating woman, and that our family was run as a matriarchy. This made long hair not only a sexual fetish, but also a symbol of power, and hence doubly desirable. Outwardly, of course, I suppressed this desire, pointedly ignoring the hair of the women I was brought into contact with, avoiding all mention of the subject, and treating it generally as the object of a frightful taboo.

Actually my preoccupation with long hair, since I desired it myself, was a serious threat to my feeling of masculinity. Now, though this whole preoccupation was suppressed at the conscious level, it became the continuous subject of erotic dreams. These dreams always revolved around women with long hair. I can remember one or two early dreams in which my mother appeared in this guise of the long-haired woman and was the subject of deeply satisfying erotic fantasy. More often the women were strangers, but the long hair was always present as the symbol of sexual gratification. Occasionally I even dreamed that I myself had long hair like a woman, but this type of dream was comparatively infrequent. Apparently the taboos were too strong, even on an unconscious level, for me to tolerate placing myself in a feminine position in dreams. The long-haired woman as a sexual symbol continued to appear in dreams, however, all the way into adult life. I still have such dreams. Curiously, too, the symbol still enters into waking life where it is associated with autoerotic fantasies. Even today the sight of a woman with very long hair will arouse a combination of desire, resentment, and fear, producing a state of anxiety accompanied by autoerotic impulses. This curious reaction has comparatively little to do with normal sexual attraction, for the conflict usually entails a certain amount of fear and resentment of the long-haired woman. I have, from time to time, had sexual affairs with long-haired women, but they have nearly always proved unsatisfactory and have taken on an autoerotic character in which no true intimate contact was possible. Conversely, most of my satisfactory love affairs, and most of my strong romantic attachments, have been with women whose hair was comparatively short. To me, a short-haired woman at least somewhat resembles a fellow human being for whom tenderness and affection are possible. A long-haired woman, on the other hand, is armed with a dreadful, fascinating, but anxiety-producing weapon which seems to threaten my self-sufficiency and my masculinity by stimulating my childhood autoerotic impulses. The emotional aberration I am describing is actually far more complex than would appear from this short description. Many factors enter into it besides simple sexual impulses. The long-haired woman undoubtedly appeared to me as a sort of consolation during a severe period of childhood rejection when my mother gave birth to a brother, and seemed to prefer him to me. I undoubtedly took refuge at this time in the imaginary long-haired woman as a sort of mother substitute, and this tended to produce autoerotic implications. Since I was deprived of feminine affection from my mother, I used this female image to take her place, and became, so to speak, self-sufficient—a man and woman in one, hence independent of women. Even today, extreme resentment or anxiety over almost anything is likely to produce fantasies about, and sexual impulses toward, the long-haired woman of my imagination. This peculiar mental aberration—actually a desire to achieve self-sufficiency—was one of the most terrifying features of the breakdown which led me to undertake analysis. It caused me to think seriously that I might be going insane—or, on the other hand, that I might be a frustrated homosexual.

Because this particular erotic fantasy has played so dominant a role in a very crucial aspect of my life (sex), I have been able to analyze it in some detail and trace it, with considerable accuracy, to its origin. It is, however, only one of numerous similar fantasies dating from childhood which also play important roles in my adult orientation to the world. Not all of these fantasies are as clear to me as the sexual ones. They have not submitted themselves to complete analysis.

Still, I can discern certain areas where they apply, and certain probabilities concerning them. The association between defecation and guilt is an obvious one. Somewhat less obvious is a phobia concerning insects. Large insects invariably fill me with a wholly irrational horror similar to the feeling women are supposed to have toward mice and snakes. The presence of a large insect in a room terrifies me and makes it virtually impossible for me to carry on any normal activity. I imagine that it is about to attack me. I dare not move from place to place lest I find it underfoot or crawling about my body or clothing. I am terribly afraid that I might come upon it unprepared. If it disappears temporarily by flying out the window or crawling behind some article of furniture I am terrified that it might reappear. Any knowledge of actual danger (whether, for example, it is poisonous or might bite me) is quite irrelevant to my feeling of horror. The horror is in proportion to the insect's size. Thus, a small but deadly poisonous scorpion would bother me less than a perfectly harmless but large beetle. When I am caught in a situation with a large insect and cannot get rid of it in any other way, I am forced to kill it; but the process of killing it is as horrifying to me as the necessity of living with it. Whether I smash it or use some insecticide on it, I feel in the position of a man using violence toward a fellow creature. I have a terrible feeling that the insect will take revenge on me for my act, and that the revenge will be a catastrophe for me. This feeling of guilt for my violence, and the attendant expectation of some terrible retribution even extends to other insects of the same kind. Often, after accidentally or purposely killing a wasp, for example, I have become desperately frightened of all other wasps, as though my guilt for the one act of violence was known to the rest of the tribe and that it had sworn vengeance against me.

Naturally, as an adult, I always suppress this childish horror
and try to deal rationally with the situation. The horror, however, is real, and cannot be wholly ignored. Its complete irrationality is underlined by the fact that it applies only to
insects and such similar crawling organisms as spiders, centi-
pedes, and scorpions. I have no irrational horror whatever of
snakes, rats, or mice. They strike me as being comparatively
friendly.

Dreams about encounters with insects have been common
with me since early childhood—particularly dreams about
spiders into whose webs I blunder or who threaten to attack
me. The association of insects with danger in general is obvious in these dreams. Beyond that I have not penetrated from
a psychoanalytical point of view. Mephistopheles maintains
that the spider is a common symbol of the resented mother.
Perhaps so. At the moment, however, I am only able to ask
myself why insects should have become such a powerful recurrent symbol of danger to me, and to analyze the terrible
feeling of guilt which overcomes me when I attack them. I
am always reluctant to kill an insect, particularly a large one,
or one of the extremely intelligent varieties of arthropods,
such as spiders, wasps, or bees. There is a feeling here akin
to a reluctance to commit murder—as though the insect were
a malevolent but intelligent fellow being, capable of resenting
the injustice of my act. This attitude undoubtedly goes back
to a childhood mythology in which I endowed insects with
human qualities and thought of them as either potential acquaintances or dangerous enemies.

Throughout childhood, my fear of insects was often com-
mented on by friends and relatives, who were rather amused
by this pronounced trait of character. Sometimes other children would torment me by exhibiting insects they had caught,

and watching me shiver with apprehension. My brother would even sometimes pull the legs off flies or other small insects and watch them struggle. This filled me with indescribable horror. I distinctly remember my mother explaining to me as a child that insects possessed life and were capable of suffering, and that hence, it was cruel to torture or kill them. I can also remember an incident that took place in the San Fernando Valley in California, where I lived as a child of five or six. I had heard that entomologists mount insects on pins for display in museums. Afire with enthusiasm, I got a pin and succeeded in impaling a struggling ant on it, bringing it triumphantly to show my mother. She, of course, was horrified, and delivered a lecture on my cruelty which was so vivid that I felt as though I had impaled a fellow human being. Sometime later I was playing in a puddle near the house. I had not noticed that the puddle (the result of a recent rainstorm) had flooded an anthill, and that the water was swarming with ants. Some of these climbed onto my arm and bit me more or less severely, sending me terrified and crying to my mother. This incident may have been the origin of my phobia. It occurs to me at this point that since my mother had preached to me the cruelty of killing insects, my present reluctance to kill insects may very likely involve a reluctance to assert myself in any way against my mother. This unwillingness to assert myself against my mother has been a lifelong problem and a source of many crucial conflicts. It is part of a larger pattern of behavior in which I have been unwilling to assert myself against others—especially in ways involving physical violence—and in which any such effort at self-assertion is followed by a violent fear of retribution. The most obvious example of this trait that I can think of in my past was my inability to fight with other little boys at school. I could stand up and be pummeled by an opponent, but I was powerless to raise a hand offensively against him for fear that the consequences to me might be complete annihilation. In childhood fights I was always beaten. I could make no effort to retaliate.

Associated in some vague way with my childhood fear of insects was a particular horror revolving about insects and food—or insects and my mouth. I can remember a long series of incidents illustrating this point. The earliest of them is a memory of trying to eat a fly. It must date from very early infancy, and is so imbedded in other memories of a similar type (watching my brother being criticized for trying to eat a fly, for example) that I would not be sure of it but for the fact that there is a very definite memory of a tactile impression in the mouth, and a visual impression concerning insect wings and a gray color. Apparently I was severely criticized or punished for this incident, for the memory itself brings on a sense of terror, and I have frequently experienced an extreme revulsion toward food which suggested the association of gray-silver color and membranous texture—a fish with fins, for example. Other memories along this line include fits of anxiety as a child if any small insect got into my food, or even if an insect was present while I was eating. I used even to imagine that insects might be present in my food when there were demonstrably no insects there. Any food (corn-meal mush, for example) that was liable to contain lumps, or be uneven in texture, immediately suggested the possible presence of insects and often caused me to vomit. I developed a violent revulsion against drinking milk at about the age of five, and I have never drunk it since. The revulsion followed the discovery of several curds (lumps of uneven texture) at the bottom of a glass of milk I had been drinking. I think they suggested the possibility to me of insects in the milk. At one point during childhood, even the sight of an insect, or the memory of seeing an insect, was sufficient to eliminate my appetite completely. At about six, I discovered a live tarantula on the lawn in front of our house in the San Fernando Valley. I called for my father, who caught the big spider and imprisoned it in a jar of alcohol which he placed on the mantelpiece. I would shy away from that jar before meals, and would often examine it carefully (and with considerable fright) before I went to bed. I was trying to assure myself that the horrible, hairy organism was safely inside the jar and could not possibly escape. I never succeeded in assuring myself completely, and was always rather worried for fear it would get out and attack me. Later, in San Francisco, where my family had moved when I was about six, some cousins of mine, conscious of my phobia and desiring to show that they were superior to it, actually ate (or chewed up) some insects of the "daddy long-legs" variety. I envied them their courage, but could never have been brought to such a demonstration of courage myself.

At about this same age I became well acquainted with an old German entomologist named Dr. Fuchs who was curator of the subject at the California Academy of Sciences, where my father worked. Under Dr. Fuchs' influence I actually took to collecting and studying insects, and learned something about the rudiments of insect classification according to the Linnaean system. I still retain this childhood knowledge, and can classify different varieties of insects today with considerable accuracy. With Dr. Fuchs, I made field trips, collecting insects, and learned to mount them for display on pins in boxes. This attempt to study a thing that frightened me was probably good for me. But I never overcame my horror. The fact that the old doctor could calmly eat his lunch of sandwiches while contemplating a large yucca board covered with large, drying, and half-mounted insects, filled me with amazement. And, even more amazing, I had seen the old doctor, on field trips, pop insects into his mouth when he hadn't a bottle handy and they threatened to get away. For me, it required an effort of the will to forget my entomological activities before I could think of eating. And eating anything in the same room with my insect collection was absolutely out of the question. This entomological pursuit did help me, temporarily, to overcome my fear of killing insects, but the fear was only suppressed. I had to examine and re-examine my long-since dead specimens to assure myself that they were really dead and could not retaliate against me. And, though I killed, preserved, and mounted hundreds of insects, I did so with an underlying feeling of terror. I never lost my fear of them. The peculiar spectacle I presented at this age—that of a frightened entomologist pursuing a scientific study of insects while shuddering at the subject of his study—caused no end of amusement to my friends and associates. It did, however, give me a slight feeling of added security to be able to classify and label the object of my terror according to the neat, established laws of natural science.

My relation to animals involved a different set of conflicts. I was taught to love animals from earliest infancy. One of my earliest memories—dating I think from about the age of three (perhaps it is by now only the memory of a memory)—is of a small black dog playing with me on a lawn in a small California town where we lived at the time. He was one of a long series of dogs that were my constant companions in childhood. I have all my life considered my relations with dogs just as intimate as, and often more satisfactory than, my relations with human beings. I also liked horses, and used to ride them bareback as early as the age of four or five. I was thrown by a frightened horse, however, at about the age of five, and the experience terrified me. Unfortunately my parents did not insist on my conquering this fear, and I never rode a horse again. I am not irrationally afraid of horses today, but I treat them somewhat warily. My relation to cats is also somewhat wary because I don't like to be scratched. But I like them. One thing I cannot abide, however, is to see an animal suffer, and if the suffering is inflicted by a human being I become angry to a point where I could almost commit murder in retaliation. I have mentioned dreams in which I felt a grave responsibility toward endangered dogs. I think they have their origin in a childhood mythology in which I actually considered dogs to be a variety of human being, and thought of myself as a fellow dog. I remember once or twice as an adult attending bullfights in Latin America and in Provence. This spectacle, though I controlled myself, filled me with indescribable horror and revulsion. I often caught myself wishing that the matador would be killed instead of the bull.

The serious conflicts that arose over my relations with animals were attributable to my mother. She was a great admirer of George Bernard Shaw, and was deeply afraid of contracting cancer, a disease she thought was related in some way to the eating of meat. For these reasons she brought the family up on a vegetarian diet. I can remember countless anecdotes related to me in childhood about the cruelty involved in killing and eating animals, accompanied by lurid descriptions of slaughterhouses ringing with the cries of victims. The whole business of eating meat was presented to my childish imagination as a variety of cannibalism, entailing incredible torture and anguish on the part of the animals. I could not see a lamb or a calf in a field without speculating on its mental processes, which I assumed to be those of a doomed and anxious fellow being, conscious that he was destined for the charnel house and somebody's cook pot. I could not sit down at a table where others were eating meat without half expecting a lamb chop or a steak to move and cry out in pain.

Later on, this extreme anxiety over meat eating subsided. After the family moved to San Francisco we came in contact with people (particularly my cousins' family) who ate meat. And, in a moderate way, meat was even served now by my mother at home. Apparently she had gotten over her phase of absolute vegetarianism. This produced an added conflict. People we knew, who were decent enough folk, ate meat regularly. The world in general did not seem to regard meat eating as criminal. Apparently my mother had deceived me. I liked the taste of meat, and I managed to assert myself against my mother by admitting that I liked it and by eating it at every opportunity I got. I did this, however, with a certain attitude of bravado which indicated an underlying feeling of guilt over the act. I occasionally suffered from stomach spasms and vomiting after eating meat. But it became a method of asserting my masculinity. To practice vegetarianism was to be feminine. My mother's ideas about vegetarianism had often been ridiculed in my presence by my uncle, who was an eminent surgeon and presumably knew something about dietary matters. Moreover, this surgeon's meat-eating sons were big strapping fellows, far stronger and more courageous than I, and possessing all the aggressive character I associated with the ideal of masculinity. Obviously if I was to learn to get on in the world and compete successfully as an individual free of my mother's apron strings, I must defy my mother and eat meat with the *sang-froid* displayed by the rest of the world. I have, ever since that time, been a methodical and continuous consumer of meat. But I am afraid that the feeling of guilt and the horror of retribution have never entirely left me. Consciously, I have long since ceased to worry about the matter. But certain incidents have occurred from time to time that show that the feeling of guilt over eating meat is unconsciously present, though deeply buried. I am sure that even today a visit to a slaughterhouse would produce acute anxiety. I am still unwilling to let my mind dwell on the process of slaughtering animals, and I have a horror of hunting. I cannot bear to look a domestic animal in the face while considering that I might one day eat part of it. Not long ago, during the process of analysis I felt a sudden impulse to go to a restaurant and order a tartar steak made of raw ground beef. I had never tasted this dish, and felt somehow in my anxious state that it would be good for me. I ordered it, and the waiter was at great pains to fix me a particularly large and succulent one, ice cold and decorated with anchovies and a raw egg. Before I had taken the first mouthful I knew that I had made a mistake. But, partly in order not to displease the waiter who had taken so much trouble, I bolted most of it down. That night I suffered from a violent attack of indigestion, and I was unable to eat for nearly forty-eight hours afterward. Analysis shortly afterward showed that the whole episode had been a desperate attempt to assert myself against my mother, followed by an acute anxiety attack based on a fear of retaliation.

Violence in general caused states of panic in me during the period of my breakdown, when even such things as heavy windstorms, news from the Korean War, and bloody episodes in movies caused me considerable upset. I am not sure, however, that the upset was not caused more by the fear that I might be upset rather than by the episodes themselves. I don't think that violence, as such, has ever been a cause of irrational anxiety to me, however, except during such emotional crises.

Of course, I have never had much experience with real violence, never having taken part in a war or a major catastrophe of any sort. In such near-catastrophes as I have witnessed—automobile accidents, thunderstorms, forest fires, heavy storms at sea, and terribly rough weather in airplanes—the effect on me has invariably been stimulating. I have always been too preoccupied with the emergency and with the possible necessity for immediate action, to be frightened in any submissive or helpless sense. As a rule, in real emergencies, I give an outward impression of unusual calm. On the other hand, I invariably experience a high state of panic in undertaking any major move involving choice on my own part—a decision, for example, to take an airplane trip, to appear on the radio, or even to tell a friend something I know he does not desire to hear and might resent. Moreover, I am a physical coward to an almost pathological extent. The sight of my own blood frightens me, extreme pain sometimes causes me to faint, and I don't know what I should do if I were faced with a major operation. Violence directed toward me as a child always scared me, but without bringing any *irrational* terror. (This applied to fights with other boys in school.) The *threat* of violence, on the other hand, was always more productive of panic than violence itself. But where the violence was directed by me toward someone else it almost invariably brought on acute anxiety and fears of retaliation. Curiously, as an adult, I have often felt that there was a certain unreality about threats of violence directed toward me. I have tended not to take them seriously, and have often assumed that they were not seriously meant when, in fact, they were. I can remember one episode in India when I stood arguing and calmly insulting the Indian Army while an Indian sentry was yelling at me and threatening to poke a bayonet into my ribs. It never occurred to me that the sentry might actually poke me with the bayonet, though he was obviously in a high state of emotional tension. I have moved quite confidently among rather hostile crowds of Mexican Indians, too, when my American companions were frightened. It simply never occurred to me that these emotional, but basically rather likable people, would actually do anything so unmannerly as attack me. I have considerable confidence in my ability to sway and control other people's actions by the power of persuasion. But for me to attack, physically, another person would be possible only under the most extreme provocation—say in defense of a close friend, or an animal that was being tortured. I doubt if I would lift a hand in my own defense if I felt I was alone in my fight—though this is difficult to say, since I have no experience whatever of the grim aspects of a primitive struggle. Actually the mechanism behind this problem of violence where I am concerned is simply the familiar problem of self-assertion. I find it extremely difficult to assert myself in any way. I can fight battles for others, but if I fight them in my own behalf, I am likely to suffer from powerful feelings of guilt.

On the other hand, I have always (except during my breakdown) gotten enormous pleasure from picturing myself as the hero of a story of violence. For a long period preceding the breakdown, I was a chain reader of detective fiction, consuming as many as three detective stories a week and showing a distinct preference for the most violent ones. In reading them I was able to escape completely from reality, identifying myself with the hero, and participating, in my imagination, in the most violent acts. This was during a time when my actual behavior was extremely passive, and I think the imaginary violence provided a vehicle for the hostility and aggression that I was suppressing in real life. With the advent of the breakdown, however, it became impossible for me to read a story of violence without experiencing panic. Fictional violence had provided me with the joys of aggression and at the same time had involved none of its penalties. After the breakdown, aggression of any sort seemed utterly impossible, even in the imagination. I became absolutely helpless, absolutely self-condemnatory, and absolutely unable to act at all—a situation that seemed to involve a sort of paralysis of the will.

Let me now examine the large and very complex subject of my relations with people. This is, from the standpoint of psychotherapy, the big, inclusive, and crucial source of my neurosis, and I have not yet succeeded in analyzing it completely. Vast areas are involved: The area of sex and my relations with women is one; another is my childhood relations with my family, particularly my mother and the brother who became my rival by being born when I was four years old; another involves my relations with bosses, companies, and organizations with which I have worked in earning a living; still another has to do with my normal social life, or the lack of it. All of these areas are undoubtedly related. Similar impulses and habits crisscross from one into another. In all of them there is a pattern of conflict revolving around stock pathological concepts—resentment, hostility, desire for aggression and dominance on one hand; submissiveness, overwhelming desire for affection and approval, fear of rejection and retribution on the other. It strikes me at this point, how utterly simple the basic principles of neurosis are, and how infinitely complicated the ramifications, displacements, self-deceptions, and symptomatic aberrations they assume when they take a grip on the individual human personality. I have already discussed a variety of personal aberrations having to do with such things as sexual fantasies, phobias, methods of escape, and so on. These manifestations, when I am in their grip, seem overwhelmingly real. Yet, in the course of analysis, it has been repeatedly demonstrated to me that they are only symptoms, and that the real causes underlying them are ultimately reducible to a few simple fears, impulses, frustrations, and desires that I hold in common with the majority of the human race. A neurotic like myself, living partially in a world of childhood mythology dominated by a fearsome array of primitive deities—the long-haired woman (goddess of emasculation), the hostile and vengeful insect god, the benign animal god who blames me for the unforgivable suffering I have inflicted on him—might easily imagine himself a ripe candidate for an institution. Yet all these supernatural apparitions are merely symbols which I myself created in childhood to explain or ward off fancied or actual injustices and persecutions suffered at the hands of people in real life. And though others may find my childhood mythology fantastic in the extreme, the causes of this bizarre theatrical display are simple conflicts that nearly everyone has experienced. In a way, I suppose, the more complex, inventive, and imaginative the mind of a maladjusted child, the more fantastic will be the language of symbolism he evolves to express and cope with his fears. From the aesthetic point of view the complexity of his personal mythological world may be a source of great interest. But from the point of view of therapy the symbolism is merely a mask for symptoms. The disease itself lies in a distortion of the mind due almost entirely to the child's elementary conflicts with his fellow humans.

Psychologically speaking, my life seems to have fallen into two parts, the first stretching from the age of dawning awareness at about three to the age of twenty when I more or less broke off relations with my family and went out to face the world alone. The second part is the adult part—a period of more or less continuous stress, involving great conflicts, two broken marriages, and two severe breakdowns. Obviously the central area linking these two phases involves something concerning my relations with my mother. During the first part, my attitudes toward her, though sometimes hostile on an unconscious level, were submissive and dependent on the conscious one. During the second part, my attitudes became to a certain extent overtly hostile and defiant, and a continuous battle went on to achieve self-sufficiency and suppression of my feelings of dependence. This battle was never a complete victory for me. It led to a loss of all intimate contact with my mother, but resulted in making my successive mates into substitute mothers and then repeating the act of revolting against my dependence on them—a process that made it utterly impossible for me to stay happily married. The loss of the substitute mother, each time it occurred, was accompanied by more or less complete nervous collapse. In this state it seemed above all necessary to isolate myself from the woman in question, but the self-isolation, undertaken at my own decision, entailed an almost unbearable feeling of guilt and self-condemnation, bringing on suicidal and other abnormal impulses. But let me begin at the beginning and try to analyze my relations to my mother and family in earliest infancy.

I was born in December 1903, the oldest, and for four years the only, child of parents with typical bourgeois traditions. Though my family owned small pieces of property from time to time, my father was not a terribly ambitious or energetic man, and during my entire childhood I was conscious of economic troubles. Actually we were not badly off. But my parents thought we were, and in comparison with the more successful families we associated with we considered ourselves to be poor. My father was a man of intellect, refinement, and profound education, liked by our acquaintances—an idealist and scholar by temperament, but somewhat ineffectual in his relations with the world. He drifted through a variety of jobs which were obviously beneath his intellectual capacities. He was a mild-tempered, rather sweet, conscientious man, who was very much in love with my mother and tended to be dominated by her in everything—not only in his relations with the family, but in his work, and other activities as well. I could not find in him an ally against my mother. He was as submissive in his attitudes toward her as I was. My relations with him throughout childhood and adolescence were quite passive and even somewhat distant. I was, I think, somewhat disappointed in him because of his submissiveness and lack of aggressive behavior. I emulated his love of culture and reading, but, as a model on which to pattern my behavior, he was too ineffectual to offer the requisite heroic stature. Actually, I feel, I never got to know him very well. My mother seemed to resent any intimacy between us, as though such intimacy might result in a masculine alliance against her, and this brings me to the general subject of my mother, who was, I think, a very neurotic woman.

My mother was energetic, furiously ambitious, and apt to be deeply resentful of her lot in life. She was a very beautiful woman and was much admired by all our acquaintances, both for her good looks and for her energy, ideas, and dominating personality. Her attitudes toward my father were ambivalent. She was deeply devoted to him, and her actual notions of family life and marriage were quite conventional. Another part of her, however, revolted against this conventionality. She was conscious of having married a poor man, while her younger sister, my aunt Caroline, had married a rich one, and she made a good deal of the virtues of poverty, while, I think, suppressing a certain jealousy of people who were well off. She hated her father, whom she accused of certain unfair attitudes toward her mother. She was extremely resentful that her father had not permitted her to go to college because she was a woman, while her brothers were both allowed to finish their educations because they were men. She was also extremely resentful of any suggestion of masculine rivalry. She was a violent feminist and a champion of women's rights. She was extremely anxious to prove herself equal or superior to the men she came in contact with, and was often driven to fury by the smallest remark of a slighting nature made against women in general. While her own life was a model of propriety, she was a great admirer of women like Isadora Duncan who had thrown off the shackles of feminine dependence. She pursued a career, with some success, as a portrait painter, and often showed signs of resenting her family because she felt it interfered with this career. Actually she loved her family, but she frequently expressed the thought that she might have been a great artist if she had not shackled herself to domesticity. My first definite memories of her have their setting on an orange ranch in the San Fernando Valley in Southern California where we had gone to live. The property was owned partly by my father and partly by his brother-in-law who lived in Minnesota, which we considered to be the "East." My father had undertaken the management of the place and had brought my mother and me to live there. My mother disliked the place, which was, in those days, a rather God-forsaken desert, irrigated here and there to produce crops of oranges and olives. Her duties included cooking dinners not only for the family, but for a family of hired farm workers who assisted in the work on the ranch. She had been brought up in rather well-to-do bourgeois surroundings in San Francisco, and living as a farm woman in this dreary environment was not exactly her idea of a rich existence. She fulfilled her duties, however, occasionally complaining and breaking into tears over her plight. In what spare time she had, she continued to paint. In this situation she undoubtedly took out some of her loneliness and frustration by lavishing affection on me. I was, at this time, about three years old, and my memories of the period, which are extremely sketchy, record no unhappy incidents whatever. I have a vague memory of a Mexican nurse who took care of me for a time. My feeling toward the nurse was definitely affectionate, and I remember that she had a dark skin. I have ever since had an instinctive liking and trust for Mexicans and Latins in general, and have often been attracted to dark-skinned Latin women, whom I find, on the whole, more satisfactory objects of affection than Anglo-Saxon women.

This nurse was obviously affectionate to me in the sense that she petted me and gave me a feeling of physical contact. It is a curious fact that I remember no such purely physical affection from my mother. Either through hostility or through awkwardness, her physical approach to me was always a bit harsh. I can remember hard hands with stiff, unyielding knuckles being laid on me by her. Probably she had resented my birth. Many subsequent impressions confirmed this idea; and, as I have said, my mother was obviously a very neurotic woman. It is perhaps from this source that my adult sexual longings and approaches never took on much tactile character, though the example of others led me to simulate tactile behavior. All my life, women have appealed to me from a more or less purely visual standpoint. I have, of course, desired sexual union with them, but not physical contact—or, more exactly, only such physical contact as is necessary for sexual union. There have been exceptions to this behavior, significantly with dark-haired Latin women who resembled my Mexican nurse. But in general the most powerful sexual stimuli I have experienced as an adult have been visual. I am no voyeur. Other people's sexual activities have never interested me. But when I am attracted to a woman it is primarily because of her appearance.

My first crisis occurred at the age of four, when my mother went to San Francisco to give birth to a second child, and took me along with her, leaving my father in San Fernando. This evidently was a very crucial event for me, and from it dates a whole series of violent symptoms. The first of these that I can remember was a nightmare that took place during the time my mother was away from me in the hospital. I was staying with my grandfather and grandmother in an old home they occupied on Pierce Street. I cannot remember the content of the dream—only that I awoke screaming, convinced that the quilt of my bed was covered with swimming fish. My cries brought my grandmother from her room carrying an oil lamp, and she even woke up my grandfather in her anxiety to calm me. I think it may have been the first time I had ever slept in a room by myself. It is the first nightmare or nocturnal crisis that I can remember. Subsequently I was to suffer from nocturnal fears and insomnia during an entire lifetime. I preserved a great affection for years, however, for the old home of my grandparents. My mother disliked it, but for me it was always a symbol of peace and security compared to our home. For many years I also retained a great affection for one of its inhabitants, my aunt Caroline, a widow with a round face and dark hair who had been my mother's rival.

My mother and I and my baby brother returned soon afterward to San Fernando. I am conscious of the problem of sibling rivalry, and am aware that I may be overstressing the point in my attempt to explain my behavior during this period. Still, there were many episodes that might easily have been attributed to such rivalry. I disliked my baby brother intensely, and used to delight in pushing him over during his early attempts to walk. For this I was repeatedly reproved by my mother, who often predicted that someday he would grow big and take revenge on me. I was already somewhat reserved in my manner toward people, and I became frightened of many things, always rushing to my mother for protection. I think I may have been trying to assure myself of her affection. I remember discovering the picture in the dictionary showing the human skeleton and the flayed man demonstrating the muscular structure of the body. I asked my mother what these pictures were, and was informed that they were pictures of "human bodies." I thereupon became so terrified I dared not enter the room where the dictionary was unless my mother was present. I used to wake in the night in a severe state of anxiety and call to my mother. When she awoke and answered me I would explain that I was afraid of "human bodies." Finally my mother pasted paper over the illustrations in the dictionary. But I still knew what was under the paper, and I was terrified for many years afterward, imagining skeletons under my bed, and often working myself in a state of panic in which I lay awake for hours. At about the same time somebody—possibly my mother—was recounting the old horror story about the bride who played hide and seek on her wedding night, locked herself in a chest with a snap lock, and could not get out (her body was discovered, I believe, some twenty years later). I overheard this narrative and became horrified.

I was unable to be alone in a room containing any sort of box or trunk. I expected the lid to move, rise slowly, and disclose a corpse. This horror of closed boxes and chests persisted for many years, and only disappeared completely during adolescence. All during this period I ran to my mother for consolation. Often I was afraid the minute she was out of the room, even in broad daylight. And I formed the habit of calling out to her whenever I awoke at night, to assure myself that she was in the room to protect me. I think I retained the habit of calling out to her at least until the fairly advanced age of nine or ten. And even at that age, going to bed alone in my room caused enormous anxiety, with sweating and insomnia lasting sometimes for hours. Significantly, I never called out this way to my father, though occasionally, when sleeping in the same room, I would wake my brother in order to assure myself that another living being occupied the room and that I was not alone with my awful fantasies.

The grisly inhabitant of the locked chest took on several forms. She became a sinister figure that would move about my bed in the night, making me afraid to open my eyes lest I see her. When I did open my eyes, in my half-asleep state, I would see her grinning at me surrounded with other "human bodies" among the shadows around me. She even had a musical motif—a note repeated and then followed by one a half step lower. I think it may have been derived from the sound of the whistles on the trains that passed in the night through the San Fernando Valley. I could conjure this sound up in my imagination at will, so that it seemed I actually heard it—and once I convinced myself that I heard it I knew that this horrible apparition was in the vicinity. Even up to adolescence this sound—real or fancied—was enough to bring on a powerful state of terror when I was alone. As I think of it now, I was deeply afraid of being alone even in broad daylight up to the age of ten or twelve, and, on walks in the woods, I would often become afraid and make my way home as rapidly as possible. At night, of course, these horrors increased proportionately.

There is a muddled state on awakening in twilight—or so I found as a child—when the darkness seems to dance with a thousand ripples like those on the surface of a lake. These ripples detach and combine, forming vague shapes and then dissolving again. Almost any object in the imagination—a ghost, a skeleton, a menacing figure with a weapon—can be discerned in their various combinations. Real objects, such as a chest of drawers or a chair, can be seen, dimly, to move or oscillate like things perceived in a thick fog. Figures of quasi-human shape can be seen sitting on top of them, grinning evilly and making hostile motions. The setting is so much a function of the imagination that one conjures up the most frightening visions. In fact, it is what one most dreads seeing that one actually sees. One's imagination seems to be detached from oneself and in league with one's tormentors. One thinks, "Wouldn't it be terrible if I saw a human skeleton sitting on that chair and grinning at me?" and behold! There it is. One tries to control one's mind and imagination, but they seem to be out of reach. In fact, the more one tries to convince oneself that the image one dreads is not there, the more certain it is to appear. One seeks to get rid of the presence. In later life I learned to get out of bed and threaten the presence with physical damage, using not very original expressions of contempt and anger, such as, "Get the hell out of here!" This was, I found, a good method of getting rid of it. But it required a back-to-the-wall kind of fighting spirit—an attitude that, no matter what the odds, I was going to smash the intruder to bits. At the time I am writing about, when I was six or seven years old, only a cry for help to my mother, and her answer that everything was all right, would reassure me and dissolve the threatening presence. I spent many hours of each night wide awake trying to control the hostile and devious demon of my own imagination. I am still a confirmed insomniac. Nowadays my waking periods are more apt to concern real problems. But occasionally, even now, after a nightmare or a restless sleep, the old-style visions will reappear. I no longer shake my fists at them. Somewhere around the age of twenty-five I found the fist-shaking slightly comic. When I see such apparitions today (and I do so frequently), I am more apt to try to engage them in conversation with some such ploy as, "Well, old boy, are you a pure fake or have you got something to say to me?" They never say anything. They just disappear.

Among the other "advanced" ideas my mother practiced in San Fernando was nudism. The theory was that people should grow up naturally to accept the human body, male or female, as a matter of course. The notion, I suppose, was sound enough. We used to play stark naked in the back yard in San Fernando. My mother herself would sometimes appear naked, and she convinced a family of neighbors that their children should join us in this *Rousseauesque* rite. One of the neighbor's children was a little girl, and it was thus that I discovered, at about the age of five, the difference in biological structure between little boys and little girls. This information caused me no embarrassment, and, as a matter of fact, seemed rather interesting. The sight of my mother's forty-year-old (and, to me, aging) body gave me, on the whole, a rather unsympathetic view of the attractions of the mature female form. Later, my mother's habit of hiring nude female models to paint, made me quite accustomed to women without clothes, and I have consequently had very little curiosity about the subject as an adult. The neighbor's little girl, however, did have one characteristic that interested me greatly—beautiful long red hair. She may have been the origin of my fetishism pertaining to the subject. I was now about six. My brother was two, and I had acquired, in addition, a little sister aged one, and a second brother aged approximately zero. I and my two-year-old brother had "Dutch cut" hair, and I was getting to the age when masculinity demanded my hair be cut short. I was deeply humiliated when tradesmen, passing by, would say, "Hello! Are you a little girl?" But I had great admiration for the long red hair of the neighbor's little girl. Finally I went to my parents and suggested either that they cut my hair short or let it grow long like a little girl's. Here again was the infantile preoccupation with what I imagined to be the female sex organ. Shortly afterward my hair was cut short, though my brother's remained at "Dutch cut" length. I have, once or twice in my life, experienced vaguely homosexual dreams concerning my brother. Perhaps they have some relation to the relative length of our hair during this period.

III

While I was still six years old, the entire family moved to San Francisco. This move marked the beginning of several great environmental changes for me, and the complexity of what I now have to describe is somewhat baffling. Within the next six years I attended several schools; I had to cope with the budding problems of sex considered as a social rather than an infantile autoerotic concept; I was faced, for the first time, with problems of self-assertion and compromise in relation to boys of my own age (I had never previously had any male friends); I was launched, in a rather childish way, on a musical career, and by ten had already appeared publicly in the capacity of an infant-prodigy composer and symphony conductor. I shall therefore refrain from any attempt to describe the colorful aspects of life that make for interesting reading, and confine myself to incidents related to pathology. To simplify problems let me attempt to divide my descriptions into categories: 1) the general situation of my family, economi-

cally, and so on; 2) matters pertaining to general social relations; 3) matters pertaining to sex; 4) matters pertaining to
career. I shall arbitrarily demarcate the period I am about to
describe as stretching from six to thirteen years old. I pick the
latter age because at thirteen I entered high school and started
a somewhat different phase of development.

At the opening of the six-to-thirteen period my family inhabited a flat on Lyon Street in San Francisco which was
owned by my great-grandmother, an incredibly aged figure
who was then about ninety-eight years old, and who lived
alone, carrying on her affairs with considerable spryness and
intelligence, though she was so old and so deaf that I hardly
had any sense of personal contact with her. In the course of
a year or so we moved to the beautiful suburb of Sausalito,
where we lived in an old country house belonging to my
grandfather. We also occupied, for a time, another house in
Sausalito belonging to my well-to-do uncle. Not until I was
about ten did we have a home of our own, which my father
had acquired in a trade of his Southern California orange-
ranch properties. It will be seen from this that we had the
status of poor relations. My father got a job as an accountant
in a bookstore. It paid very little, and there was always a pinch
in the family finances. This particularly disturbed my mother,
who resented (and at the same time made a virtue of) our
poverty. (Her relatives continued to be fairly well off.) The
situation was intensified by a family tragedy. My little sister
died suddenly at the age of three, of tetanus, which she had
contracted from a sliver of wood while playing in the back
yard. This tragedy affected my parents deeply. It troubled me
also, but I think most of my reaction to it was caused by sad-
ness at seeing my parents so deeply crushed. I had at the time,
of course, no conception of death as an event of human con-

sequence, and I had somewhat resented my little sister while she was alive. The cause of this resentment was my mother, who had always wanted to have a little girl (I think she would have preferred me to be a girl) as an ally in what she felt to be a hostile masculine world. I can remember her pride in my little sister, her delight when my little sister asserted herself more or less violently against her brothers, showing signs of resisting the power of the male of the species, and her general feeling of having succeeded in thwarting the male sex somewhat by having produced a female offspring. I was subjected to lectures about the superiority of women over men, with my little sister being held up as an example. Naturally, I resented this, and it produced toward my little sister the ambivalent combination of affection and hostility that has always characterized my relations with women.

This combination of affection and hostility toward women was played upon by my mother in curious ways. She appeared to be delighted by my dependence on her, and apparently foresaw no danger in keeping me tied to her apron strings. Already at seven or eight I began to think of this bondage as unmanly, and, indeed, judged by the standards of the few fleeting male friends I began to make at this period, it *was* so. I deeply resented my mother's lectures on the superiority of women over men. But my mother had me trapped. Every once in a while she would ask, very earnestly, "Do you know what Abraham Lincoln said?" "No," I would reply submissively, though I knew very well what Abraham Lincoln had said; I had heard it often. "Abraham Lincoln said, 'Everything that I am, everything that I hope to be, I owe to my mother'"—a touching tribute by a masculine, rail-splitting country boy who became President of the United States. But pronounced by my mother to her outwardly submissive offspring, it seemed to be a proclamation of eternal debt, and every time the phrase was repeated it caused hidden resentment accompanied by fear. It was amplified by such folk proverbs as "A boy's best friend is his mother," which had a similar effect. Any passing display of immaturity—say, a boy of seven or eight playing with children's blocks—would bring visible pleasure to her face. I continued to be dressed in infantile clothing long after such garb should have been left behind. Obviously my mother didn't want me to grow up and become a man. Later on, when I was first introduced to the opera, the penultimate scene in *Cavalleria Rusticana* where Turiddu cries "Mamma! Mamma!" was, I found, regarded by my mother as an edifying example of filial piety. I don't think she realized that Turiddu was about to be slaughtered by the Teamster whose beautiful wife, Lola, he had made overtures to. Turiddu, in her mind, had obviously been fooling around with other women, and, finally, he had returned, in his mind at least, to "Mamma"—which was as it should be.

But I am getting ahead of my narrative. Social relations begin, of course, within the family. I have described my relations with my three-year-old sister. Those with the still younger brother were closely affectionate and have remained so to the present day. He was the only member of my family to whom I was able at that time to feel an absolutely unqualified attachment. My father, during this period, was usually at work, and I saw him only on weekends, when he would occasionally take us on little trips to the beach or to the country. My four-year-old brother (the original sibling rival) showed at this time marked signs of the growing hostility and tendency to aggression that he developed to a remarkable degree prior to adolescence. He was the bad boy of the family. He was openly hostile to my mother, while I was outwardly compliant and submissive. He was also very hostile to me, and used to grasp every opportunity to torment me. He was, at the same time, a great adventurer. He got into scrapes with the neighborhood children. He stole things. He misbehaved at home. I suppose he felt rejected. But his method of showing it, unlike mine, was aggressive. I deplored this, and gloried in the fact that I was a good little boy while he was a bad one. But I resented the sort of feminine position in which this attitude left me. A good little boy was a little boy who did what his mother told him to do, but it was already beginning to dawn on me that good little submissive mama's boys were not admired by the world outside the family. I was beginning to become aware of what is known as the American "sissy syndrome." My brother might be "bad," but he was no sissy. I was "good," but my goodness tied me to my mother's apron strings. Secretly, I think I admired my brother's capacities for violence and misbehavior. And it was also evident to me that my mother loved my brother fully as much as, or more than, she did me, in spite of his hostility and my compliance.

My first encounter with school was a terrific adventure in unexplored territory, and I reacted to it as I always do to such adventures, with intense anxiety, and in this case, floods of tears. I was taken to school by my mother, and was somewhat resentful at being accompanied by her, since it deprived me of the feeling of courage and independence that the other little boys, who came alone, seemed to have. When my mother left me there, however, I felt completely abandoned in a strange world, and my first reaction was to weep publicly in class. Having thus made a public spectacle of myself, I became very much ashamed. My schoolmates, however, did not treat me with the scorn I expected. I explained my outburst to them on the grounds that I felt sick, and this explanation having been given some credence, I soon found myself making friends among my associates. On the whole, I began to like school immensely. My mother's inhibiting influence was absent. I was among equals. I found that I could compete with my colleagues quite successfully in certain subjects. I began to develop a distant admiration for certain little girls in my classes, and feelings of close friendship for some of the little boys. My stay at this particular school, however, was short. The family moved to a different location, and, for a period, I was away from school again. During this period my mother was somewhat scornful of public schools. She had a rather snobbish sense of family solidarity and was determined that her children should not grow up to be ordinary ones. She was very critical of school teaching in general, and maintained that she could give her family far better instruction at home than they would receive among the vulgar mob. It seems never to have occurred to her that it is the chance of social contact, fully as much as the education, that makes a school a valuable institution. She did not encourage social contact at all. While I was attending school, I was not encouraged to bring my friends home. A pattern of family behavior was being set up which lasted for years. The family, under my mother's domination, was a close-knit unit, self-sufficient and more or less hostile to, and critical of, the rest of the world. It was a very special family, perfect in outward appearance according to my mother's lights, and destined for supreme distinction. While she emasculated her male children unrelentingly, she was very proud of her offspring and their accomplishments. An unavoidable rash or pimple on the face of one of her children was regarded by her as a crime on the child's part. Hadn't she brought us up on a refined and nourishing vegetarian diet? What right had we to break out with the skin eruptions that afflicted the rest of humanity? Little boys who ate meat and happened to have sallow complexions were pointed out to me as examples of what could happen without the requisite sort of nourishment. I thought they were dying. Once, I remember, at the home of some people we were visiting in Berkeley, my mother's insistence that her children were second to none had a really dismaying consequence. There was a small swimming pool on the place, and while the children of the people who owned it were paddling happily about in the cold water, I, who was unfamiliar with the pool, remained seated on the edge, testing the temperature of the water with my foot. This was not enough for my mother. She kicked me into the pool where the other children were showing their superiority by swimming. The result was a certain amount of gasping on my part followed by a flood of tears. I had not performed heroically as my mother expected me to do. Any tendency I had at the time to dependence on my mother's apron strings was intensified by these attitudes about the family's exclusivity and superiority. And with this dependence there was already beginning to grow in me a deep resentment against the family. The resentment was unconscious and suppressed, for my dependence and my fears of being disloyal did not permit me to recognize its existence.

Our feeling about our neighbors in San Francisco was extremely distant. As far as I remember we never had any of them as visitors, nor did we visit with them. The family next door was studying how to play ragtime on the piano. My mother was very scornful of this. She regarded ragtime as vulgar. She had meanwhile taught me the rudiments of piano playing. I played waltzes by Chopin. I also regarded ragtime as vulgar. My brother, however, when he took up music several years later, made a point of learning how to play ragtime pieces on the piano, and insisted on pounding away at them whether she liked them or not. My brother also showed a healthy aggressive tendency to make friends with the neighbors. He had several close companions, both boys and girls, who played with him on the street around the corner. (He was now about four, and was already accumulating more social experience than I, who was already eight.) As for me, I stuck close to home, occasionally visited my uncle's family (about whom I shall presently write at considerable length), went a few times to Sunday school at a Swedenborgian church on Lyon Street, took some French lessons at the Alliance Française, and helped my mother with cooking and the dishes.

For a short time, at the age of eight, I was also permitted to attend a kindergarten run by an elderly German maiden lady named Miss Steinman. My fellow students ranged in age from three to six, and I stood out among them like an elderly oaf. Miss Steinman was good to me, however. She treated me with special respect, and, while the other children did cut-out puzzles and played with blocks, she taught me, in a rudimentary way, to speak and read German. I found this slight acquaintance with the language of great value in later life. My German pronunciation, formed early, has always been quite good. But this was, after all, a kindergarten. I could make no contact with the children in it. They were infants.

Fortunately I was sent to school again, this time a big San Francisco grammar school on Washington or Jackson Street. Again I found that I liked school immensely, but again my stay was short, perhaps a semester. I was now a bigger boy (about eight or nine) and had to face larger problems in competition with others. Here occurred my first physical combats, with practicing young sadists. They were, with one exception, complete defeats for me. I simply stood there, trembling, and allowed my nose to be punched until it bled. After that I would return home, or go to my teacher in tears. I dared not raise a hand in retaliation. To make things worse, my mother, instead of encouraging any combative impulses in me, would complain to the teacher, who would take a few disciplinary steps toward the boy who had beat me up. Thus I was dependent for protection on authority and was placed in the position of teacher's and my mother's pet. This, of course, brought further violence from the other side, and I was, for a period, beaten up nearly every day. The pattern of the attack was always the same. The tough guy would approach me saying, "Wanta fight?" I would not dare to say "No." I would just stand there until a well-aimed punch would down me with a bloody nose. Later, I became rather friendly with my tormentor, and admired him greatly. On one occasion I managed to retaliate against the aggression of another little boy who attacked me. But I dared not use my fists. I attacked him by kicking his legs with my feet until he retired in defeat. The method was unorthodox and was frowned upon. It worked, but it was not really successful as a method of aggression. I was ashamed of myself, and apologized to my victim later. The only other vivid memories I had of this school were of a schoolmate who collected stamps and became my friend, encouraging me to collect stamps too, and of a very pretty little girl with long curls whom I fell in love with. I never dared speak to the little girl, however, and there was another little boy who was much better looking and more self-assured than I, who often talked to her. I remember thinking what a handsome couple they made! (We were all about seven or eight.) Any real competition with this fine specimen seemed out of the question. So my love remained distant and unexpressed. In any case, I was soon taken out of school again. The family moved—this time, I think, to the suburb of Sausalito—and I lost whatever social contacts I had made. Again my education reverted to my mother, who did teach me reading and writing, elementary arithmetic, some drawing and piano playing. I was sent, at about this time, to study piano and musical composition with a private teacher, a rather inhibited but kindly English organist named Wallace Sabin. My mother paid for the lessons by painting a portrait of his wife. I never became very proficient as a pianist, but I became interested in writing music, and produced some childish compositions, which gave my mother the wholly erroneous notion that I was a musical genius. At about the same time, my brother took up the cello, for which he showed immediate aptitude, and soon he was a much better performing musician than I. My parents, from this time, began thinking of retrieving the family finances by making us into child prodigies. I was made to feel that I owed my parents an incalculable debt for bringing me into the world and making sacrifices for me. One way in which I could pay off this debt was to become an infant-prodigy musician and make lots of money for them. I showed signs of resenting this idea of the family of *Wunderkinder* from the very beginning, and I hated being asked to play with my brother before people. This, however, belongs to a different section of my narrative.

One of the greatest assaults ever made on my budding sense of masculinity by my mother was my enforced attendance at dancing school during this period. I was not only required to participate in what was known as "ballroom" dancing (which was onerous enough at the age of seven or eight); I was sent to "fancy" dancing classes in which there were very few boys, and in which one was required to practice ballet steps among throngs of little girls. My more assertive brother was also sent to these classes. He reacted more or less violently, turning his toes in when he was supposed to turn them out, making enormous efforts not to learn anything, and sometimes hiding behind articles of furniture and refusing to participate at all. I myself reacted as usual. I submitted to the indignity and did my best to interest myself in this shameful feminine business because my mother wanted me to do it. But the suppressed resentment this caused was a fearful thing. I can feel it today as I write about it, and even now it is almost impossible for me to appreciate the humor of what was, actually, a pretty funny situation. My mother seemed almost deliberately sadistic in her desire to force my submission to this feminine occupation. She used to maintain that boys should learn to be as graceful as girls—another ramification of her militant feminism and resentment against the dominance and all the characteristics of the male sex. But I never dared to revolt overtly. I went to each class with a deep sense of shame and foreboding. I dreaded each session, and left it afterward with a feeling of relief and gratitude that I had survived the ordeal. Never, however, did I express my sense of outrage to my mother. I think she even had the impression that I enjoyed this activity. The time when the male ballet dancer could be regarded as a fully masculine athlete was then far off, at least in San Francisco. Outside the classes I deliberately attempted to walk and move as awkwardly as possible and to stand with my shoulders hunched forward in the most graceless position I could conceive. I still retain vestiges of this passive revolt today. They express themselves in a round-shouldered, pipe-smoking, hands-in-pockets appearance which, to me, is an expression of masculinity. If anybody today (particularly a woman) accuses me of being physically graceful or sensitive (actually I have rather feminine aristocratic hands, of which I am ashamed), I take the remark as a mortal wound, and seldom see the person again. For many years I have clung to an inner picture of myself as a large, muscular, rather awkward man who, to me, represents the masculine ideal. It does not, of course, accord at all with my physical appearance, which is slight, thin, and small. But it still expresses itself in a rather heavy walk and a habit of stooping forward as if I were compelled by my great height to look downward in order to communicate with the rest of humanity. Frequently as a child I was told to stand erect in order to correct my tendency toward round shoulders. I always deeply resented this command, and never obeyed it. People wanted me to look graceful. I'll be damned if I will, even today. I'd rather die a hunchback than submit to what seems to me a feminine ideal imposed upon me by my mother.

Submerged among these masculine resentments, there was one peculiar pleasure I took in these dancing classes, and this was the opportunity to observe, and have personal contact with, girls. I was deprived, however, by the nature of the situation, of a thoroughly masculine orientation toward them. I was in the humiliating situation of being, so to speak, one of them. The little girls in the dancing classes fascinated me, but I could not approach them assertively as a male. I was, in this particular environment, completely deprived of my masculinity.

My principal male companions during this period were my cousins, the sons of my uncle the surgeon, children with whom I had an affectionate, admiring, and also somewhat envious relationship. In every way they represented the ideal of aggressive masculinity that I felt to be so lacking in myself. They were comparatively wealthy, while I thought myself to be poor. Their father owned two automobiles, while my father had none. They were self-assertive, physically powerful, and willing brawlers and fighters, while I was inhibited, small, and cowardly. They owned a yacht on which they sometimes took me sailing on San Francisco Bay. Where women were concerned, they were healthily contemptuous. They treated their mother with outward respect, but outwitted her at every possible opportunity. They scandalized the maid in their home by lifting her skirts and making obscene remarks to her. The only way I could possibly compete with them was on an intellectual and imaginative level. They considered me a profound scholar, and had great respect for my brains. Actually, I can see in retrospect that they were rather neurotic too. The older boy, in particular, obviously suffered from feelings of rejection. But his neurosis, unlike mine, expressed itself aggressively. In this, they were like my brother rather than like me. From the outset they took a protective attitude toward me. I was submissive, nervous, and the admiring emulator of their more modest feats of self-assertion. They fought my enemies for me. They dared to do things that I was afraid to do. Our relationship was, on the whole, close and congenial, but it left me always in the passive and cooperative role. Their admiration for my intellectual powers was, of course, better than no admiration at all. But it was not an admiration for the qualities that would have assuaged my greatest need—the need to be demonstrably a male. At no time during this period did I find the possibility of competing against any male friend as an equal.

When I was ten years old my mother conceived the idea of making me into a great violinist. It was, by then, obvious that I would never become any great shakes as a pianist, and she had recently been enormously impressed by attending a concert by the handsome and able French violinist Jacques Thibaud. So a violin was bought for me, and lessons were arranged with an Italian named Giulio Minetti who was a distant relative by marriage of my surgeon uncle. He also taught one of my cousins the violin. I was not able to pay his full fees, so it was arranged that I should help him with odd jobs around the studio, copying and marking sheet music and so on. Meanwhile I continued my work in piano and composition with Mr. Sabin. Mr. Minetti was out to make the most of his new pupil, and when he discovered that I had written an amateurish composition for orchestra, he decided to present me publicly as an infant-prodigy composer and conductor. He was, at this time, conducting an organization known as the San Francisco People's Orchestra, which gave rather mediocre symphony concerts in the Civic Auditorium. He proposed that I appear as a guest conductor, conducting my own composition. In order to accomplish this design, he had my sketchy composition considerably improved and re-orchestrated by another Italian musician. There was a rehearsal at which I managed to correct certain details (I knew the improved score by heart). Then came the public concert in the enormous, drab auditorium. Six thousand people sat applauding as I strode to the podium dressed in a sailor shirt and knickerbockers. My knees were shaking. They stopped shaking, however, as soon as I took up the baton. I gave the initial downbeat and the piece began.

I do not think that there is any exercise of power in the military, financial, political, or sexual spheres that compares with that of an orchestral conductor, who, at the slightest flick of a baton, can induce an immediate response from a professional orchestra of a hundred men. And once tasted, this power is like the flavor of human blood to a man-eating tiger. He must find it again. I know of men who have spent vast fortunes—either their own or their wives'—to become symphonic conductors. I know of other men who have attached themselves, in virtual slavery, to great composers or to reigning operatic divas, in the hope of becoming conductors in collaboration with them. I also know of men who have become composers in the hope that their celebrity as such would bring them to the conductor's podium, where they remain, forgetting all about their compositions. I daresay that if all biographical mysteries were brought to light, it would turn out that men, here and there, had committed murder to become conductors. And here was I, a ten-year-old boy in knickerbockers, exercising this power over an orchestra of men, most of whom were five and six times my age. Every movement of the baton made an instant effect on the sound that arose from the orchestra. Indeed, I found that I had to be very careful with my motions, for fear that the effect would be too great. The fact that the composition was not a very good one and that much of it had been rewritten, was of no importance in the light of my sudden accession to power. The power itself was the thing. Hang the composition! The press responded with publicity, and I became, in a minor way, a civic celebrity. Mark this moment! It lasted only a week or so, from initial rehearsal to press interviews. But it was a turning point. Its influence lasted for many years. For one thing, the event, more than any other in childhood, oriented me toward a furiously ambitious musical career. In my helpless search for a method of distinguishing myself, I had suddenly found a way. I could not assert myself in the social sphere, but here, falling into my lap, was a superb method of spectacular self-assertion. I could become a genius. In fact, judging by my feat and the public adulation that attended it, I already *was* one. Even today, it sometimes strikes me that this experience on the podium as a ten-year-old composer-conductor was the peak of my career, and that everything subsequent to it has followed a steady downward course.

Now that I can look back over most of a lifetime, I can see how crucially the incident affected my behavior. My one method of asserting my ego, the thing into which all the frustrations of childhood channeled, the one thing which seemed to redeem me from hopeless inferiority, my one outlet—to be a genius! I remember a conversation with a high school chum that occurred a few years later: "I am going to be a genius when I grow up," I told him. "Why?" he asked casually. "My God," I responded, "don't *you* want to be a genius?" "Not particularly." The answer left me dumbfounded, and a little contemptuous of my chum. It seemed incredible that any reasonably intelligent person should have no ambitions to be a genius. I could conceive no other satisfactory way of life. Eight years later I was playing the violin in a professional symphony orchestra and composing symphonies. It had already occurred to me by then that I might conceivably go down in history with less stature than that of Beethoven. But I was supremely confident that I would soon be acclaimed as one of the greatest symphony conductors in the world. Eleven years later I came to the end of that rope. Being a symphony conductor, I found, entailed much more than I had bargained for—not only talent, not only knowledge and technique, but also the capacity that I had always lacked for asserting myself in normal social relations. Conductors must be men of the world and politicians, ready to seize and create opportunities just as businessmen or society doctors do. They must be ready to become acquainted with the "right people." Later on, in my early twenties, I experienced a severe nervous breakdown. It had several evident causes. Perhaps one of them was this conflict between ambition and practical aptitude. At any rate, one of the outcomes of this breakdown was the abandonment of music as a career. Curiously—or naturally—the symptoms of this breakdown entailed a sudden return of all my childhood fears of total inadequacy. Again, at the age of twenty-two, I became a little boy of nine, harassed by feelings of inferiority, horrified by feelings of femininity, conscious of an aching void left by the absence of my mother, yet deeply resenting her for helping to betray me. My one and only channel for asserting my ego had failed. Slowly and painstakingly, rising from the total helplessness of acute neurosis (this time without psychiatric help), I had to create another channel. Fortunately, I had some of the resilience and optimism of youth to help me in the task.

But to get back to my narrative: My early efforts to embark on a career of being a genius met with serious encouragement on the part of my mother. She never apparently felt any impulse to laugh me out of my bizarre and unrealistic notion. I think my father would have sensed the danger, but his ideas carried little weight around the house. Moreover, there were conceptions about life then current in California that lent a certain credibility to the idea. The place was full of infant prodigies. Lots of people expected to be geniuses someday. Californians had always combined a certain boundless optimism with the cultural arrogance and lack of hard realism characteristic of a provincial area. The idea that one's son might grow up to be a Beethoven or a Toscanini seemed rather natural. To deride such an idea seemed the height of cynicism. And my mother was no cynic. As it was, my furious efforts to redeem my maladjustments by practicing the violin were applauded. And the violin cut off even further my already sparse contacts with the world about me. While other little boys played baseball or fought for equality among their friends, I practiced my fiddle, secure in the certainty that it would someday make me superior to them all.

This situation, which might well have, and almost did, head straight to the madhouse, was relieved by certain factors. Thanks be to God, I was not cut off entirely from normal human contacts. At the age of ten, shortly after my sensational appearance as a symphony conductor, I was permitted to enter school again. I also joined the Boy Scouts of America, and though I was somewhat frightened by the barrack-room atmosphere in which my scout troop held its meetings, I did manage to make a few fast friends among them. My mother, however, did not encourage these friendships. I seldom had the temerity to bring my schoolmates and scout friends home, and when I did, my mother frequently found fault with, or ridiculed, them. They were, obviously, not destined to become geniuses. Our sights in the family were aimed far higher than theirs.

Again I found that I liked school. This time it was the State Normal School on Duboce Avenue, a large, airy institution filled with attractive student teachers and a vast polyglot gathering of children. I entered school this time, not with trepidation, but with a high feeling of adventure. I was, as before, a very good student. This time I was also a much bigger boy, and I found that my relations with other boys of my own age were considerably more civilized. It was no longer necessary to have my nose bloodied in physical combat to establish contact with my schoolmates. They were old enough to regard fighting as a somewhat unsatisfactory method of social intercourse, and those boys who insisted on pursuing it were looked down upon by the majority. Brains began to count for something, and since I was by nature a man of brains rather than a man of brawn, I began to reach a somewhat better adjustment to society. I began to be intensely interested in literature and writing. In fact, even from this age, reading, and little stories that I wrote, were far more satisfying to me than the pursuit of my musical studies. A parallel interest in writing and scholarship as a career began to develop, and never completely left me even during my days as a professional musician. I think this may have been due to my father's influence. He was a great reader, and I think would have liked to have been a writer. Our bookshelves at home were filled with calf-bound volumes of old classics—Plutarch and Herodotus, works of German philosophers like Schopenhauer, Kant, and Friedrich Schlegel, comparative moderns like Dickens and Thackeray. From this library, I also got more escapist types of literature: the works of Dumas and Jules Verne, which I devoured with a degree of excitement that was almost frantic. My father, who was an extremely well-read man, used to discuss books with me, and encourage my reading. My mother, on the other hand, seemed to resent my bookishness somewhat. There were several possible reasons for this. In the first place, my excitement during the reading of things like novels of Alexander Dumas, *père*, was so intense that I would emerge from them glassy-eyed and obviously overstimulated. In the second place, if left to my own devices, I probably would have done nothing but read. It was the perfect escape from the problems of real life. In the third place, I think my mother resented my father's habit of burying himself in books, felt that he would have accomplished more in life if he had spent less time reading, and was afraid I would grow up to be like him. Also, I think she resented my possessing a habit that brought me into a somewhat exclusive intimacy with my father, an intimacy in which she did not participate (she was not much of a reader herself). At any rate, she took the attitude that any great amount of reading was a waste of valuable time, and whenever she discovered me buried in a book, she would interrupt me and set me to a less agreeable task—washing the dishes, sweeping the floor, or practicing my fiddle. I formed the habit of outwitting her in this battle. I would memorize my violin exercises, and then place a volume of Sir Walter Scott or Jules Verne on the music stand, reading by the hour while to anyone's ear outside the room I appeared to be practicing diligently. I felt rather guilty about this deception, however, and always kept one ear cocked toward the door listening for my mother's approaching footsteps. I had arranged the book so that it could be quickly closed in an emergency, leaving an innocent piece of music on the stand before me. My reflex to my mother's approaching footsteps became so acute that I would jump guiltily and collect myself when I heard them, even when I didn't happen to be reading. My attitude toward the violin was rather hostile from the beginning. I never liked the instrument, and I still dislike it today. But I was determined someday to be a great symphony conductor, and I felt that violin playing (and eventual entrance into an orchestra) would be a step toward this goal. My progress on the violin during this period, however, was not extraordinary, and I loathed playing it before people. I was also somewhat ashamed to be seen carrying a violin case on the street. In San Francisco, a city that had emerged only about forty years before from a frontier psychology, it was the badge of a sissy. To add to this problem, my brother, who had started his cello playing earlier, was a much better cellist than I was a violinist, and my mother was at continuous pains to stress this fact. According to her, he played with "feeling," while I scratched abominably. Well, in a sense I can hardly blame her. I can today imagine few more excruciating experiences than listening to an unskilled student trying to play the violin. Actually, I never got to play the violin with much satisfaction even during my professional years as an orchestra musician. I suffered always from dismaying attacks of stage fright, and I could never face the idea of playing it as a soloist. This attitude was unquestionably the product of a deep, lifelong resentment against being a violinist. I was studying the violin more or less patiently and methodically as a step toward being a conductor. Later, when I found myself frustrated in this ambition, I felt an overpowering necessity to rid myself of the profession of violin playing. It was still, at the age of twenty-two, the mark of my mother's power over me. After a few years more of playing because of economic necessity, I gave the violin up altogether. Today I have not touched it in twenty-five years, and have no desire whatever to do so.

At the State Normal School, meanwhile, I continued the enjoyable business of getting acquainted with my fellow man. School was an entirely different world from home, and, on the whole, a much pleasanter one. The two worlds did not converge in any way. My mother never came in contact with my school friends, and I never brought them home. At school, I was an individual, reasonably self-reliant and able to choose my contacts without parental domination. From this situation, I think, arose a peculiar split in my subsequent emotional life. I never confided my adventures in school to my mother. School was my world, and she had no place in it. One of the main features of this world was the opening realm of sex, considered as a social phenomenon.

My father, through some inhibition or other, had never discussed the subject of sex with me. My mother had hinted at it, but the picture she gave me was concerned with childbirth, and it was a horrifying picture indeed. According to her, children were brought into the world through incredible suffering on the part of women, and there was a strong implication here that I owed her an incalculable debt for the torture she had undergone in giving birth to me. Men were involved in some way in this process of childbirth, but just how was not explained. Later, I learned from school friends some vague and inaccurate notions of the process of sexual intercourse. But the whole subject was suffused with an atmosphere of mystery, danger, and guilt. From the resulting misinformation and from my curious probing, I gathered that good little boys did not practice sexual intercourse, and that if they did, it was only in the duly sanctified state of marriage. Only by a lifetime of devotion, obviously, could a man repay a woman for the unbelievable martyrdom of childbirth. And sex, as I had discovered, had something to do with childbirth. At the age of ten, the sexual urge had not yet become insistent, and so the whole problem remained, for the time being, somewhat academic. Later, however, the attitudes formed at ten became the basis of severe conflicts.

Though the physical aspects of sex were fraught with these terrific dangers, there was no taboo concerning its idealistic aspects. The novels of Sir Walter Scott, in fact, made idealistic sex a highly laudable, desirable, and important phase of life. In fact, I can, without exaggeration, say that I learned about sex from Sir Walter Scott. The sex I learned about was highly symbolic. One needed a lance and a white steed (both obvious sexual symbols in the world of the Freudian unconscious), and one searched continuously for women in distress, dispatched the dragons, ogres, or other Oedipal father symbols who were menacing them, and then rode off with them sitting on the forepart of one's saddle. The imagery was faulty in one respect—one does not seek out a woman simply because she is unhappy or in dire circumstances. But otherwise, Sir Walter's nineteenth-century metaphor was fairly apt. The trouble with it was simply that it was a metaphor. Anyhow, from the age of ten, I became a great idealistic lover. I would never, for a moment, have considered confiding to my mother how I felt about women. I was afraid of being ridiculed by her. I was afraid she might try to interfere. There was also a strong feeling of resentment against her which made me unwilling to admit to her that I was attracted by women. After all, she too was a woman, and the admission to her that I was capable of being attracted by any woman implied an acceptance of female domination. So my love life remained a complete secret from her—something carried out on an inspirational level in the outer world of school, where she had no place. I think that probably the fundamental factor in this situation was, again, my simple desire to be a male. I had never been a very successful male in my mother's company, and any idea of asserting my masculinity in her presence, or with her knowledge, was out of the question. With her, I was still a child, but once I was at school, away from her emasculating influence, I could assert my maleness as a free and equal member of society.

The first object of my love was one of my teachers, a pleasant, curly-haired Italian woman named Catherine Vercelli. I say woman because she did not seem to me a girl at all, since she was so much older than I. I imagine she was about nineteen or twenty. For a period of months, I lived for the pleasure of attending her classes, where I would sit looking at her with calf-eyed adoration. At night I would lie awake conjuring up the memory of her. I remember that she used to wear a corsage of violets over a black lace bodice (or whatever it was that women covered their breasts with in those days). She also had freckles. Her hair, like that of most of the women I idealized, was comparatively short and kinky. I did not do particularly well in her classes. I was too absorbed by her looks and personality. She liked me, and with the intuition of a mature woman, she guessed the state of my emotions. When I misbehaved slightly in class in order to be held after school hours for punishment, she knew that it was because I wanted to be alone with her. These after-school sessions were among the most delicious moments of my life. She would give me some perfunctory task to do, and then dismiss me with considerable warmth and affection. I can still remember my intense excitement as she approached my desk, radiating a wonderful aura of highly charged female magnetism, bending over me to examine my work, and brushing my cheek with her sleeve, quite aware of the effect she had on me. Once she was teasing me about my behavior, and said to me, "You know, all men have their vices—drink or gambling or something. I think yours is going to be women." What a heady tonic to a ten-year-old! What balm to my long-suffering masculine ego! Miss Vercelli, bless her soul, was treating me like a man, admitting she found me attractive, not for my brains or my fiddle playing, but just for my qualities as a male. That afternoon I went home in a joyful state resembling complete mental paralysis. Though I had said nothing, I had achieved for the first time that intimate avowal of a mutual feeling of affection between man and woman, which is perhaps the most mysterious and exciting of all human experiences. Shortly afterward my affair with Miss Vercelli came to a graceful and painless end. She left the school after bidding me a sentimental little farewell. Later I discovered that she had left to get married, but by that time she was only a memory.

Having found that I could inspire affection in the opposite

sex, I now developed an insatiable hunger for it, and cast about deliberately for a suitable object. I soon found one again, this time in a girl of my own age. Winifred Schultz had a face that smiled easily, blue eyes, and, again, short, curly black hair. But she acted as though I did not exist. It now devolved upon me to be the aggressor. The assumption of this role frightened me greatly. I was overcome with feelings of inadequacy. I had no idea how to approach her, and I was deeply afraid of being ridiculed by her. For some time I simply sat in class looking at her, unable to make a move of any kind. Clearly the situation called for a spectacular feat of some sort on my part. I must enlist her attention by some extraordinary move. I had a small toy printing press at home, and this seemed to provide the answer. With some trepidation, and working in deep secrecy, I set up the words "I love you" in type, and printed a number of calling cards with this inscription. I then carefully burned all the cards but one, and took this one to school with me, leaving it on her desk. This procedure had a certain advantage. She didn't know who had left the card. If, on reading it, she broke into gales of laughter, I would pretend it was left by somebody else. But, to my delight, she read it somberly and secreted it in the bosom of her dress, looking shyly around to try to discover who had sent the message. Her eyes finally lit on me, and I guess my expression of mingled hope and anxiety gave me away. Anyhow she smiled and nodded conspiratorially at me. After class, she waited for me outside the door and we held a rather halting and incoherent conversation climaxed by a shy kiss. To my amazement, she was quite serious about the whole thing. She didn't think it presumptuous or silly for me to have done what I had done. I had learned another thing about women. When you talk to them about love, they don't laugh at you.

On the contrary, they are apt to take you very seriously in-deed. And the idea that the calling card was a mechanically produced object, which might have existed in quantity, never occurred to either of us.

I don't remember precisely what happened to this romance afterward. I saw Miss Schultz rather infrequently, except in class. I think I accompanied her to a couple of school affairs. Since we were both far too young to approach the idea of physical consummation, even on the "petting" level, there was no place for the romance to go after the avowal had taken place. Shortly afterward Miss Schultz must have left the school. In any case she disappeared from my life. But she had established a pattern which I followed for many years after-ward—too long, in fact—for my relations with women re-mained on an idealistic plane up to the age of twenty. From my contact with her I discovered that I was really happy only when I was thinking and romancing about a woman. This sort of romancing offered a remedy for every sort of anxiety and depression, and a complete escape from the realistic as well as the frightening fantastic aspects of life. When I was harassed or miserable, I deliberately looked for a girl to fall in love with, and I fell in love with premeditation, because I knew that it would make me happy. Of course, all these ideal-istic attachments were plagued at times by jealousy, feelings of inadequacy, and so on. But the sufferings I underwent as a lover were nothing compared to the loneliness and frustration I felt when I was without a girl. Since the physical side of sex was unthinkable, these encounters became the basis of power-ful imaginative fantasies which took on the character of ro-mantic fiction. I lay awake nights, inventing heroic stories in which I rescued the girl from enemies, became an important and famous man in order to lay my achievements at her feet, and so forth. There is, of course, a certain element of ego-centricity about this stage of erotic development. I never understood, or even tried to understand, the personality of any of these girls. I never treated any of them as human beings. To me, they were wonderful apparitions who had the power to make me forget my troubles. And the whole focus of my emotion was really turned, not toward the girl, but toward myself. It was I who had to be improved and endowed with superhuman, heroic characteristics in order to be worthy of the girl. It never occurred to me that she, too, had problems and frustrations, or even biological urges, or that she had to do mundane things like taking a bath or going to the toilet. To me she was the possessor of superhuman perfection. I would not have been satisfied with less. And, of course, what I was in love with was not really a girl at all, but a figment of my own imagination—a part, so to speak, of myself. This female image, which transferred itself successively from one girl to another, became a permanent part of my psyche, and bedeviled much of my subsequent life. At the period of which I am now speaking—from ten to twelve or thirteen years old —the image was a psychic refuge and an icon of enormous power. For example, my early childhood fears—of the dark, of insects, of "human bodies," skeletons, the dead woman in the trunk, and so on—would all disappear the minute I was in love with the image. I even gave up crying out to my mother in the night. The act seemed unworthy of a hero, and I had to be a hero to deserve the girl. But beyond this, the act was no longer necessary. I had found an object outside my mother to depend on for solace. Among its effects was a tendency to stimulate my ambition. I was now prepared for heroic exploits. I studied hard, to improve my intellect; I rose spectacularly in the ranks of the Boy Scouts of America. I read the

Bible extensively, dressing myself romantically like a priest in an old black dressing gown belonging to my father. I fancied myself a great philosopher, and actually read Kant's *Critique of Pure Reason* from cover to cover without understanding a word of it. I read treatises on military strategy, imagining myself a general, and accounts of exploration, imagining myself a great explorer. I became avidly interested in a huge variety of subjects ranging from archaeology to chemistry. I discovered a talent for writing, and wrote large quantities of rambling stories and poetry. All of the poetry was written to girls. All of it was terrible, but it served to impress the girls with my virtuosity, and indicate to them that I was a very out-of-the-ordinary fellow. Meanwhile I became conscious of my appearance. I strove to look dignified and knowing. I could not tolerate the slightest imperfection in my complexion or the way my hair was combed. I spent hours regarding myself critically in the mirror. Socially I was, I am afraid, somewhat of a snob and a boor. I used to make statements to my friends that had no point whatever, and then chuckle to myself as if their meaning was very subtle and cryptic—way above the heads of my listeners. I discovered that this bluff usually worked, since I had a certain reputation for brains, and people were easily convinced that what I said was profound even though its meaning eluded them. So I got a name as a great wit and humorist, in spite of the fact that my witticisms were incomprehensible both to my audience and to me. The violin, I continued to practice in a desultory way, out of a sense of duty, and with a vague (and during this period rather abeyant) hope that it would lead me to the symphonic podium.

A curious attachment to religion, or what I imagined to be religion, appeared during this period. I had been brought up by free-thinking parents, and had been inside a church only once or twice in my life. I had, however, been impressed by the grandeur of religious ceremony, and some impulse led me to emulate it. I have written of my solemn readings of the Bible, clad in my father's dressing gown. But I have not mentioned my construction in the sandy, cramped basement of our home in San Francisco of an idol before which I performed rites and sacrifices, usually involving small bits of food which were afterward eaten by ants. The idol was made of plastolene stuck to a wooden skeleton, and it looked something like a pre-Columbian or other primitive image. It had thumbtacks for eyes, and a modeled nose. Below the shoulders its construction was elementary. It had no arms and legs, just a torso. Its name—derived, unless I am mistaken, from some novel by Dumas—was "Exili." With the help of a flashlight, I tended Exili day after day with rites, and I think I really believed that these secret ceremonies had a bearing on my good or bad luck. Not much of a religion for a boy whose Episcopalian parents had long since left the church and brought up their offspring outside it. Still, Exili satisfied some craving of my moony preadolescence—perhaps merely a need for the dramatization of those scenes in old abbeys that I had read about in the novels of Scott. That I was practicing idolatry never entered my mind. My position was that of a priest of a secret cult whose membership consisted solely of myself.

Moreover, at this age I first became conscious of a certain dualism in my personal cosmology. It seemed obvious to me that the world I inhabited might well be a dreamlike illusion, and that there might be another world in which I existed part of the time. I was beginning to think metaphysically and to question the nature of reality. Fantasy and reality were equally real to me, and fantasy had become by far the preferable realm. The art of music, in which I was deeply involved, expressed itself in a world that bore only a tenuous relation to the real one. Perhaps this had something to do with my mental convictions. But they went beyond music. I was convinced that my physical body and I were two different things. My body was a generally patient but sometimes uncontrollable animal which, like any other animal, flourished when it was treated well, and occasionally became unruly. True, I lived inside it. But I was not a part of it. I merely had to go to sleep in order to rid myself of it. It seemed to be a temporary habitation to be used in the waking world. I suppose that I was stumbling on the body-and-soul concept that is common to most established religions, and that I was developing, prematurely, into a mystic. At any rate, the dual nature of my universe appeared quite real to me. I remember at one time discussing the curious nature of reality with one of my muscular and masculine cousins. He seemed deeply troubled. He did not want to understand. "If you think like that," he said, with some finality, "you'll go off your nut." (Nut, in those days, meant "head" or "mind.") My cousin was firmly rooted in reality. He did not welcome any idea that questioned it. He was like Dr. Johnson. If you kicked a stone, it was there. I, on the other hand, had already cast my lot with Bishop Berkeley. I was rather surprised, in a later conversation with my father, to find that he viewed the world in pretty much the same way as I did. I was not only surprised; I was reassured.

Of course, I often descended from my dream-reality dualism and participated a bit in normal social activities with other boys. But I never played games. The competitive aspect of baseball, football, and even such things as hopscotch, was repellent to me. Such healthy competition endangered my security by threatening to make me a potential loser—to demonstrate that I was subject to the same weaknesses and defeats as others were. I have never in my life enjoyed a competitive game or sport, and I avoid them even today. Moreover, at this time, I tended, rather dangerously, to prefer my own company to that of other boys. I was quite happy in solitude, and sociability in general was surrounded with fearful problems—dangers of inadequacy and rejection—which made it, on the whole, an unpleasant experience. I felt quite unworthy of meeting the world unless I could do so with a complete confidence in my spectacular superiority to it. Vestiges of this attitude have remained with me all my life.

During this period my relations with my brother were extremely hostile. He apparently resented my tendency to isolate myself and my pretensions to scholarship. Whenever he found the opportunity, he would molest me with a hundred little tricks, all calculated to disturb my peace of mind—putting insects or stones in my bed at night or beating tin pans outside the door of my room while I studied. He was now seven or eight, and was beginning to equal me in strength. Often these minor harassments grew into rough physical battles in which it took all my strength to subdue him. In fact, I never did succeed in subduing him completely, for the minute I let him up off the ground, he would be at me again with disruptive tactics. I was not really afraid of him (even though he once or twice threatened me with axes and knives), for I was still considerably stronger than he. But his gadfly strategy made it almost impossible, at times, for me to concentrate on anything, and I never seemed able to gain any authority over him. The final tribunal, in these battles, was always my mother, who dealt out punishment as best she could, but who could not allay our fundamental hostility. His resentment of me undoubtedly arose partly from a resentment of authority in general. But there was bad blood between us on other counts too. I had followed my practice of pushing him down as an infant, with all sorts of methods of cheating him and getting him to do menial tasks for me in return for promises I never fulfilled. In attacking me he was expressing many long-standing grudges.

One of these promises by which I had exacted servitude or peace and quiet from him had been the guarantee, somewhere around 1911, that if he did as I wished, I would give him a certain number of nickels in 1915. That was a magical date, set for the opening of the Panama Pacific International Exposition, and all San Francisco was looking forward to it. The debt of nickels continued to pile up. Sometimes, in order to gain his compliance, they had to be offered in scores, even hundreds. When 1915 came around (somehow I expected it never would) I was, of course, without the nickels to repay my stupendous debt, and my mother referred to the situation solemnly. Clearly I had been dishonest. My brother's gleeful harassments increased. I don't blame him. I deserved punishment. Another ploy of mine had been to threaten my brother with excommunication if he didn't do as I liked. The words of the excommunication were, "If you don't do this you can't belong to the club." This worked for a time. But the club consisted only of myself and my youngest brother, and it was soon noted that the threat of excommunication had no real effect. I was playing, for the time being, on my brother's very real fears of rejection. A great deal of his wayward behavior as a child, I can see now, was based on these fears and on the desire to attract attention at all costs, even if the attention proved to be hostile.

As far as I can make out, I had by the age of thirteen acquired nearly every basic personality problem that I carried through life. Many things happened to me after that, but the pattern of my reactions continued to follow paths that were already fixed. As I look back at it all today, it is quite obvious to me that a great part of my personality still remains at the thirteen-year-old level of development, though intellectually I have, of course, broadened my knowledge and interests. I am today regarded as something of a sophisticate, but my real reactions to society and the world are still as full of fears as they were at thirteen. I have had numerous affairs with women, but my reaction to women continues to be clouded with all the infantile habits of mind I had at that age, and I have never been able to reach a really satisfactory relation with the opposite sex. Why did my emotional life remain arrested at that point? Is this something that happens to most people? From observing them, I don't think so. Well, at any rate, it has happened to me. Let me try to analyze the reasons. Perhaps the history of the next few years, from thirteen to the age of eighteen when I entered the San Francisco Symphony as a professional violinist, will throw some light on the problem. I have at this point, however, a vague feeling that I have already described my complete psychological development, and that from now on I shall have nothing to record but a series of incidents to which my reactions are more or less predetermined. Nevertheless, let me make the attempt. At least I can record what happened to me outwardly, and perhaps some of these happenings will prove to have had more of an effect on me than I imagine.

At thirteen, I graduated from the State Normal School, and went, diploma in hand, to be duly enrolled as a student at Lowell High School. I was, as usual, somewhat frightened by the new adventure. To make things a little easier, my be-

loved aunt Caroline accompanied me to the door of the school.
I was glad it was not my mother, for now I had begun to resent
her domination so deeply that I disliked being seen in public
with her. From the first, I became an enthusiastic student,
taking special interest in English literature, history, geometry,
and biology. Latin and algebra, I found more difficult and
less interesting. My natural facility for writing made me a
prize pupil in English classes throughout my high school
period. In this subject I became a sort of virtuoso, reading far
beyond the requirements of the curriculum, and associating
myself with several eager students with the same interests. I
patronized the public library and the library of the old Me-
chanic's Institute downtown on Post Street. The amount of
reading I absorbed during this period was colossal. I read
methodically, going through whole literatures, with a great
sense of scholarly accomplishment. I would read, for example,
the entire collected works of one author, like Victor Hugo,
then branch out into most of Balzac, some Flaubert, nearly all
of Anatole France, and then acquaint myself with the work
of a whole company of minor French authors, like Alfred de
Vigny, Théophile Gautier, and Emile Augier. I would go
methodically through the Elizabethan dramatists and became
well acquainted with Ben Jonson, Beaumont and Fletcher,
and Marlowe, as well as Shakespeare. I ransacked the early
Anglo-Saxon epics, the German romantic philosophers, the
Greek dramatists, the *Iliad*, the *Odyssey*, Plutarch, Livy, the
Morte d'Arthur, Goethe, Dickens, Thomas Hardy, some of
Tolstoi and Dostoievsky, and a vast amount of American literature. I virtually wept over Tennyson and some of the German romantics like Fouqué (*Undine*). I became enchanted
with the literary elegance of a little volume of collected essays
by Addison and Steele, virtually memorized their eighteenth-

century idiom, and patterned both my literary style and my speech on it. I became a rather elegant and artificial writer and talker, and, with a few similarly inclined chums, I used to hold extremely learned discussions on literary matters. There was a certain snobbery about all this. I would pride myself on my knowledge of obscure authors, and venture, with a great sense of superiority, into the most abstruse volumes of philosophy, reading them with great patience, though often, I failed to understand them clearly. I think there may have been, in all this activity, an impulse to emulate my father, who was a widely read man, and to get even with my mother, who had frowned upon my reading habits at an earlier period. Anyhow the education I got in the process was considerable, and has since been of great value to me in the absence of college training. The habits of reading that I formed at that time persisted throughout life. I am, even today, an instinctive scholar.

My family lived at this point in a six-room flat in a two-story house my father owned on Duboce Avenue. It overlooked a small park, called appropriately Duboce Park, and the house had a back yard which my mother planted with box hedges and flower beds. The six rooms were a bit crowded for the five people who lived in them. My brother the cellist practiced in one of the two rear rooms, which was also used as a dining room, and he slept there too. My parents' bedroom, in which I myself had slept up to about the age of ten, and in which my baby brother also slept, was alongside. Facing the street, there was the front and back parlor arrangement, with sliding doors, which had been fashionable a few years before, and there was an extra room at one side which my mother caused to be thrown together with the parlor by removing the intervening partition. She did her painting in the room thus created, clos-

ing the sliding doors. I practiced my fiddle and did my studying in the rear parlor behind the closed doors, and after the
age of ten I slept there too. When my father came home from
work, the sliding doors would be thrown open, and he would
read the newspaper or a book there, or help me with my Latin,
a language he was familiar with from his law studies. The flat
was nearly always in disarray, with unmade beds and un-
washed dishes (my mother scrimped on housekeeping in order
to devote more time to her painting), and when the doorbell
rang there was a hysterical attempt to put things in order before the front door was opened and the place was revealed to
the eyes of friends, relatives, or strangers. The flat had its ad-
vantages. It was within walking distance of both the State
Normal School and Lowell High School. And the park offered the younger children a place to play during those rare
hours when the family was permitted to indulge in recreation
with other children. Often the whole family went on outings
to Marin County or near those lakes which are at the south-
western edge of the city—then a comparatively wild area. But
these outings were strictly family affairs. Contact with the outside world was limited to school and an occasional meeting
of the Boy Scouts of America.

My mother, at this time, I think, considered herself to be in
a state of rivalry with me. She pursued her career as a painter.
Occasionally she dropped remarks that were obviously motivated by resentment, about my lack of understanding of human feeling and sentiment. She would hold up my brother
as my superior in this respect, and point to what luscious
emotional effects he drew from his cello. (She conceived him
to resemble her side of the family while I resembled my father's.) Where my brother was concerned, this was pure
poppycock. He had about as much human feeling as a pirate.

He simply played a more pleasant-sounding instrument, and played it better than I did the violin. But there was perhaps some justification for her opinions about my lack of human development. I was escaping from life into literature. Her methods of stating this attitude, however, aroused my resentment. It seemed again as if she were urging on me those feminine virtues of gracefulness, sentimentality, and so on, which I was now resisting with every masculine fiber I had. On the other hand, the attitude of exclusivity and superiority of accomplishment that she had bred into me still affected me powerfully. I became one of Lowell High School's highbrows. At one point I even had the arrogance to wear a flowing Windsor tie to school, and to persuade some of my highbrow colleagues to do the same as a badge of their superiority to the common herd. This produced several minor lynching parties in which our neckties were ripped off and tied to lampposts and fire hydrants. All of this, however, was done in a spirit of high good nature, and actually I managed to hold a respected position among my schoolmates, and was, on the whole, considered a pretty bright fellow.

It was characteristic of me, however, that I never sought any position of power among the students that involved an element of rivalry. I would never put myself up, for example, to run for the office of class president. I was desperately afraid of rejection and defeat, and it was conceivable that I might be defeated in an election. So I tended to seek appointive positions, and to exert my power in ways where it was not threatened by competition. For example, once during elections for class president, I decided to demonstrate my power by picking a rather unlikely candidate and forcing him, by a campaign of publicity, into the post. I would never have dared run for the post myself, but I was certain that my powers of persuasion were so great that the mass of students would elect anyone I endorsed. (This was another example of my old childhood inability to fight my own battles, and my corresponding assurance that I could be successful when defending anybody else. I simply had to have allies.) My hunch proved to be right. My candidate, a nice inoffensive fellow of whom I was secretly somewhat contemptuous, won the post by a large margin, and subsequently appointed me editor of the class paper—a fine demonstration of practical politics in which I was the maneuvering power behind the throne. I have all my life sought this sort of power, while avoiding the responsibility of high office myself. At the same time I have always had a sneaking envy of the extrovert whom I have helped to the high office. I would have liked to bask in the honors and trappings of the great. But something has always prevented me from seeking these trappings. I think it is a fear that I might ask for them and be refused. The possibility of such refusal is something that I cannot face. In my dealings with adolescent clubs and gang organizations, I was never the leader, but always his advisor and confidant. I could have been a prime minister but never a king, a party organizer but never a president. The responsibilities of leadership exposed me to hazards that were too great. Kings and presidents can be deposed and defeated by popular opinion, and I have always had a deep fear that people, in any quantity, would reject me. This trait followed me conspicuously into adult life. It had a great deal to do with my failure to become a symphonic conductor. There was a point, at about twenty-two or -three when a career as a conductor was not out of the question. I was even given an opportunity or two to conduct orchestras, and could easily have created others. But I failed to accept the opportunities that were given me, and seemed utterly unable to push myself forward. I was deeply afraid that the orchestras would consider me inadequate and that I might be laughed off the podium. The chances of this happening were actually quite remote, and even if it did happen there would be no reason why one could not try again. But I was so afraid of the possibility of rejection that I couldn't even bring myself to make the attempt.

I could probably have been spared this experience of impotence in my chosen career if I had cultivated sports early in life. Participation in competitive sports teaches one a vital lesson which I am only just beginning to learn after more than half a lifetime—that it is no disgrace to lose. It also teaches one to rely to a certain extent on chance, and to accept bad luck for what it is rather than picturing it as a sign of total disaster and inadequacy. But I never entered sports in school. My fear of defeat and my dislike of uncertainty made them all onerous to me. Such gymnasium activities as I was forced to participate in, I hated. Even today few sights are as distasteful to me as that of a gymnasium locker room full of sweating athletes, flexing their muscles and rubbing themselves down. I hated the very act of undressing and putting on a gym suit and tennis shoes. It made me feel naked and vulnerable. I was ashamed of my physical body. I was slightly built and had skinny arms and legs which I didn't like people to see. At one point, when I was about seven, I had attempted to make my arms bulge with muscularity. I read avidly a series of articles in one of Mr. Hearst's papers by the then reigning champion of the ring, Jess Willard. The series was entitled "How to have health and muscles like mine." It prescribed certain exercises which I performed dutifully. But my arms remained as skinny as ever. I had never been able to compete physically against anybody as a child, and as an adolescent I had lost all desire to attempt such competition. I would go through Swedish drill and breathing exercises dutifully, but when the whistle blew for a basketball game, and the other boys rushed joyfully to their places, I would cringe, and try to find some way to avoid participating. I was afraid of making mistakes and being ridiculed. I was awkward in catching and throwing balls (to throw a ball badly had been, in childhood, the mark of a girl). I wish that, at this time, some athletic instructor with a knowledge of psychology had sensed my plight and taken me in hand. I would, actually, have considered it a great achievement to have developed some prowess at the simplest game. But this did not happen. Once I discovered that skinny little fellows were good at fifty- and hundred-yard dashes, and I devoted some little effort to track training. I always wore myself out, however, in my efforts to better my running time, and at the one track meet in which I participated it rained heavily before my race arrived, and the affair was called off. I was greatly relieved at this development, because I was literally shivering with apprehension at the idea of competing. The rain relieved me of the charge of cowardice. After all, I had shown up and offered to compete. But I felt just as I had as a child when I stood my ground and let the tough little boys bloody my nose. I hated to be called a coward, but I also hated to make an aggressive move of any sort. No sound was more welcome to me than the bell that signaled the end of the gymnasium period. It meant the finish of an hour of frightening violence, competition, uncertainty, and anticipated humiliation.

Military training was altogether different. The United States had entered the First World War a year or so before I arrived at high school. The war was now at its height, and Junior Reserve Officer's Training Corps had been formed in

all such institutions. There was at least a battalion, equipped
with uniforms and rifles, attached to the school, and I joined
it at the first opportunity. Here competition was not a matter
of physical strength, or of pitting myself as an individual
against my colleagues. The possession of uniforms and guns
made us all equal. In uniform, through some sort of pride, I
stood up straight and threw back my ordinarily hunched shoulders. Moreover, the techniques of rifle drill, parade forma-
tions, target shooting, and so on, fascinated me. I soon had
the U. S. Infantry Drill Regulations by heart. Often we were
called upon to march in public parades. I was a very good
soldier. I got promoted successively to corporal, sergeant,
quartermaster sergeant, company top sergeant, battalion sergeant major, second and first lieutenant, and captain. At one
summer training camp session I reached my military apogee
as regimental adjutant. I was intensely proud of my climb
through the stages of the military hierarchy, delighted that
other boys had to salute me, and fascinated with what little
I knew of the military life. My uniform gave me an enormous
feeling of importance, and being entrusted with so dangerous
and manly a weapon as a gun (Craig rifle, vintage 1903, I
think) seemed a great and exciting honor. It is a wonder
I didn't decide then and there to pursue the military life. I
didn't realize at the time that the very reason I liked it was
that it offered an escape from competition, a sort of guaranteed
security and a predetermined pattern of life that would in-
sulate me from many of the problems of the world. My father,
for once, had the good sense to make himself heard on this
point. He had never had a very high opinion of militarism
and of the military mind in general. He greeted my military
honors with gentle cynicism. He was more interested in my

development as a scholar, and went out of his way to help me with my algebra.

One thing this military training contributed was a certain amount of ease in talking before large groups of people. Though I was paralyzed with fright when anyone suggested I play the violin before even a roomful of people, I could address large crowds without the slightest feeling of nervousness as long as all I had to do was talk. I frequently made speeches, and lectured before groups of students with perfect ease and much gratification over my powers of ad libitum expression. My early experience before an audience as an infant conductor had also helped this feeling of ease. The reason it didn't apply to violin playing was that violin playing always represented to me, in some unconscious way, a submission to the emasculating influence of my mother. Just how deeply I hated the violin I never even realized myself at this age. The hatred was largely unconscious, and manifested itself mainly in irrational symptoms like stage fright.

My musical career received a sudden impetus, however, when I happened to fall in love with a girl who was a pianist. She was one of my schoolmates, and was not acquainted with my family at all. Her name was Elaine Nesbitt, and she played the piano quite well. She was very pretty in a buxom Anglo-Saxon way, with brown eyes, a nose that turned up and rather short, very curly blond hair. To me she became the idealized, perfect woman, and my tendency to romantic fantasy—now reinforced by a growing sexual urge—endowed her with a stature and desirability that were virtually superhuman. I remember practically talking myself into being in love with her. As usual, I wanted to be in love, for only when in love was I happy. She seemed the perfect object. She was pretty and she knew music. I could impress her with my prowess as a musician. Miss Nesbitt did not succeed in making me like the violin, but she fired me with a furious ambition to be a great musician of some sort, and since the violin was a step in this direction, I started practicing it like mad. I also began pursuing my studies in musical composition with a brand-new fervor. I devoted four or five hours a day to my musical studies. I dare say my parents were astonished. They had no idea of the source of this sudden inspiration. By organizing a little musical club at school with her as pianist and myself as violinist, I contrived to see her more often. I wrote an elaborate musical composition which I dedicated to her, sending her an inscribed manuscript copy. To my great mortification, she showed the copy to her parents, who promptly got in touch with mine and told them about it. As always, I wanted my love affairs to be carried on in complete secrecy, and I was deeply embarrassed. My mother became somewhat alarmed at my emotional state, and tried to tell me that no girl was worth all that effort. I really think she was a little jealous. Later she met Miss Nesbitt's parents, didn't like them particularly, and was at pains to point out to me that Miss Nesbitt's mother was a very fat woman and that Miss Nesbitt herself might grow up to be like her. But these criticisms did not deter me a bit. I carried on an idealistic love affair with her for five years or so. The affair, which was above any such coarse considerations as physical intimacy (beyond the point of holding hands), actually inhibited my normal sexual development. Owing to it, and my extreme notions of fidelity, I had no physical experience of sex until the age of twenty. Miss Nesbitt was apparently impressed by my accomplishments, flattered by my devotion, and amused by my rather courtly and romantic way of making love to her. I asked her over and over again to marry me (meaning, of course, to make sexual union possible). She demurred, wisely, saying that we were too young to contemplate such a step. So there was nothing for me to do but go on playing the hopeless lover and beating my brains out in attempts to astonish her with my accomplishments. Once or twice I brought her home, but I was so afraid of my mother's ridicule that I did this reluctantly. I also took her to one or two parties at my cousins' house. They found her very attractive and admired my taste in women. This I found gratifying. Outside the family, I made no bones about my feeling for her. Everybody at school knew that she was my girl. Many of my more realistic schoolmates regarded my supercharged romantic attachment with amusement. I discussed her with my closest friends as gravely as Don Quixote might have discussed Dulcinea del Toboso. As a matter of fact I read *Don Quixote* at this time, and could find nothing humorous about the old knight's attitude toward his lady love at all. I put myself in his place, and found him a very noble and high-minded gentleman. I think I sometimes vaguely sensed a slight lack of realism about my position. I knew that other boys were more casual about girls, that they were interested in obtaining physical intimacies, and sometimes got them. But it did not occur to me that these boys were on solider ground than I, and were likely to grow up to be far happier human beings. The old family superiority and exclusiveness applied here. The mob could act as it wished. Mine was a very special love affair, attuned to the truly heroic nature. Nothing like it had ever existed before except possibly among such legendary characters as Tristan and Isolde or Romeo and Juliet. This was true because I was a very special man, destined for a future as a genius. The laws by which ordinary boys and girls lived did not apply to me, and the object of my attachment was a very special woman, made out of entirely different materials from those that went into the construction of ordinary girls. How could it be otherwise?

Again, of course, I was retreating from the world and building about myself a solid wall, guaranteeing myself an illusory superiority over my fellow beings and guarding myself against competition of any sort. I think Miss Nesbitt would justifiably have considered me more impressive as a prospective husband if I had shown some talent for such average accomplishments as playing baseball or just getting along with people. But my egotism, with its attendant fears of rejection and competition, was too formidable for me to tolerate placing myself in any such light. I was afraid of being rejected by her in any open competition with other boys. I had to overwhelm her with unique and unprecedented feats.

IV

VI

In my efforts to tilt at windmills, I finally tilted myself into a career I fundamentally disliked, and worked myself into a lifelong state of neurosis as a consequence. Miss Nesbitt moved away to Portland, Oregon, when I was about fifteen and a half, but this did not lessen my ardor. I corresponded with her for years, writing the most impassioned and flowery love letters, and telling her of my accomplishments. Despite my hostility and general lack of aptitude, I became, by sheer force of will, a pretty good violinist. I can remember a stage, at about seventeen or eighteen, when I realized that I no longer had any idea what Miss Nesbitt looked like. But by this time she had become a career as well as an object of love. I kept her image enshrined by the same sort of main force with which I drove myself in my musical studies. The abstract idea of her very existence assumed the proportions of a religious fetish. It was unthinkable that I should be unfaithful to her. Heroes and geniuses like me were not unfaithful

—or so I thought. My entire self-respect, my ambition, my way of life, were all intertwined with the idea of her. Several times I nearly drifted into sexual affairs with other girls. My sexual appetites were strong. But I always stopped myself before any consummation occurred, with the thought that I was, after all, dedicated to this ideal woman. By this time my love letters to her were taking on a highly artificial literary flavor. They became hard to write, and were actually too flowery to be sincere. But I continued forcing myself to write them. My whole way of life seemed to depend on it. My ethical values, supported by a formidable ego, reinforced my untenable position somewhat as follows: It was good to be faithful, evil to mess around with sexual affairs as other boys did; it was good to accomplish great things, evil to fall behind in one's fight for superiority and uniqueness. I became a professional violinist in the San Francisco Symphony at eighteen. I became a conductor of theatre orchestras at nineteen. At about this time I learned that Miss Nesbitt had gone to Paris to continue her musical studies. At twenty, I, too, was taken to Paris by my family to study. Of course, I went to see Miss Nesbitt. Of course, after five years of separation, she did not remotely resemble the image I had been carrying around in my mind. She was still a very attractive girl, but she was a different girl. I still tried deliberately to recapture my original emotion. I pretended, even to myself, that I was in love with her and wanted to marry her. Again, wisely, she put me off, noting that I was still a student with a career before me. I think she would have submitted to sexual relations with me at this point. Several hints she dropped confirmed the idea. But sexual relations with the image of my dreams—or what was now its human relic—still seemed out of the question. I was still a virgin, an egotist, and a prude. I soon left Paris for Vienna to tilt at more windmills. I had never really been interested in Elaine Nesbitt as a human being, and that was what she had turned out to be. The illusion was at an end. Within a year I was carrying on an affair with another woman, this time an affair including real sexual relations. I received a note from Miss Nesbitt asking what had happened to me. I wrote her a short reply saying that I was married. I was not, but my new affair had taken on all the obligations of marriage in my mind. The great romance was over. I wish it had been brought to a healthy finish four years before, or, even more, that it had run its course as a casual physical and companionable relationship in San Francisco just after I first met her. But I was no realist where women were concerned. Again, I had merely been in love with myself.

I am conscious that I have been using the word "love" very loosely. It is, of course, a loose word that has different meanings for different people. The particular meaning it has for me as I write this is, in fact, as far as possible from its common meaning indicating the emotion that exists between two companionable and sexually devoted people. My meaning is more like the one the word had during the Crusades and the "courts of Love" in medieval France. It denotes a peculiar fixation on the image of another being. The image that is the subject of the fixation has only a slight relation to the woman who inspires it. It is something created by oneself, and applied often at first with an effort of the will to the woman in question. It is, of course, related to sex, but its relation, in this connection, is hidden, symbolic, and mythological. It is a fantasy, but it is one that becomes attached to the woman and that becomes very powerful and durable. It is, I suppose, an adolescent phenomenon, and yet it is a phenomenon that has persisted into my adult life, where it has often led to complications. You will say that what I am writing about is not love at all. And you have a point. I have, myself, many times, experienced feelings toward the opposite sex that are of an entirely different sort—frankly sexual feelings, feelings that are more in the nature of friendship. These are undoubtedly more genuine than the romantic attachments of my adolescence and the years immediately following it. But, in general, they have never had the overwhelming power of the fixation I have described. They have been human attachments, not romantic ones. The fixation I have called love was, for me, a refuge, a religion, and undoubtedly an artificial construction meant to fill the vacuum left by my mother's absence from my emotional life. Nevertheless, the fixation remained attached to the woman in question with an adhesive force that was remarkable.

I have not, so far, devoted much attention to my relationship with my father. This is mainly because his influence over me was rather slight during early childhood and was completely overshadowed by that of my mother. The influence was there nevertheless, and in my high school years it became somewhat more overt and pronounced. I have described my father as a rather passive and ineffectual man where the affairs of the world were concerned. I can remember incidents in childhood when his lack of capacity for aggression disappointed me greatly. In his relations with laborers on the orange ranch in Southern California, he was kindly and extremely sensitive. He would complain bitterly about their inefficiency in private. But he would seldom take an authoritative tone toward them publicly, and if he did, as happened rarely, he would wind up in a highly emotional state, trembling and showing other outward symptoms that I could see. He seldom stood up to the neighbors in disputes about farm problems, and he often allowed himself to be cowed by them. Here, too, when he was finally goaded into retaliation of any sort, he suffered from severe anxiety. He was a believer in justice and reason rather than force, and he was often worsted by men whose intellectual capacities and methods were far inferior to his own. He never spoke an unkind word to my mother, and, as a result, tended to be ruled by her. Even when punishing me with a spanking, his momentary attitude of aggressive authority would bring on a great emotional upset for him, and it would be quite obvious to me that he was suffering more than I was. He was a very insecure man. When I was about six, he became involved in a lawsuit against his brother-in-law, a highly aggressive, fatuous extrovert who had blandly attempted to cheat him out of his rights to certain properties in Southern California. The business of dragging himself into court in an aggressive action against a member of his own family (his older sister's husband) reduced him to a pitiable state of nervousness and self-condemnation. The brother-in-law had acted as a sort of father to my father (whose own father had died when he was an infant), and now claimed, unjustly, that my father owed him a large sum for bringing him up and educating him as a child. The suit was over this obligation, and, since the brother-in-law's attitude was based on the rankest sort of injustice, my father won it. There was a strong element of spite on the brother-in-law's part. He hated my father. However, every sort of justice was on my father's side. He was a struggling man with a family to support, while his brother-in-law was wealthy and childless. But despite these obvious points in favor of his position, the lawsuit cost my father untold anguish. He was, in this respect, very much like myself. For him, any act of aggression brought on a terrible fear of retaliation. Earlier, I remember, the brother-in-law and his wife had visited us for a short time. He was a coarse, assertive Midwesterner with positive opinions and a loud, domineering manner. He admired my mother (though she detested him), and imagined he was the type of male who could subdue her spirit. His attitude toward my father was patronizing. He wanted us to go to live with him and his wife in Minnesota. My father and mother would have none of this, and he was piqued. We all hated Uncle Merritt, as he was called. The only good thing I can remember about him is that he once made me a present of a ten-dollar gold piece. I also remember his telling a grisly story about what were evidently a number of dismembered corpses he had come across in the basement of a big building in Chicago. Later they turned out to be plaster casts of the sort used by art students. He related this story with great glee, watching my face as it blanched with terror. Finally, and I suppose unwisely, my mother dragged me from the room. It was many months before I recovered from my fright over this episode (this was during the period of "human bodies" and the dead woman in the trunk), and I can still remember the extraordinary feeling of horror that it brought about. The patronizing attitude of Uncle Merritt toward my father aroused a fierce childish resentment in me, but I was unable to cope with Uncle Merritt. The whole situation left me helpless, with a mingled sense of loyalty toward my father and a feeling of disappointment in him for his ineffectual attitude. I very much wanted my father to be a hero, and unquestionably he was not. Later in San Francisco, my father got a number of jobs at which he was poorly paid and generally imposed upon. I can remember him frequently upset by financial worries and what he considered acts of deliberate humiliation on the part of his bosses. Even a slightly disparaging word from his superiors would cause him to brood for days, and he was quite incapable of talking back or retaliating for these (probably imaginary) insults. My mother often criticized him, gently but definitely, for his lack of spunk and ambition and his general inadequacy in coping with the world. In the absence of a positive drive from him, I suppose it was up to my mother to provide all the family initiative. Now that I think back over the situation, it occurs to me that perhaps I have blamed my mother too severely for my childhood upbringing. After all, somebody had to seize the reins if the family was to survive, and my father seemed incapable of doing it. I am not sure but what my neurotic childhood was as attributable to my father's extreme passivity as to my mother's extreme aggressiveness.

On the other hand, there were admirable features of my father's nature which invited my affection and respect, and even my reaction to his ineffectualness was one of mingled pity, sympathy, and vague worry. He made sacrifices for his family, and drove himself through many an uncongenial task to support it. He was a man of great charm in social matters, handsome, sensitive, gallant, and much admired by women. He was, by nature, an aristocrat, with polished manners and immaculate habits of dress. He was a fluent and often brilliant talker.

He had, moreover, passed through a fairly heroic phase at one time. The trouble was that this phase had preceded my birth, which took place when he was already in his forties. He had left the University of Minnesota, without graduating, and had become a prospector and miner in Arizona, where he had first met my mother. Later on, in search of a fortune, he had participated in the Alaska gold rush. But his adventures had brought him no profit. He returned from Alaska as poor as before. What I admired most about him was his learning, his respect for knowledge, and his ability to think. This was one field in which he was unquestionably my mother's superior. During my high school period, when I was away from my mother to a certain extent and able to indulge my love of reading and scholarship, I found my father a sympathetic intellectual companion. He discussed the contents of books with me—often philosophical ones—and gave me my first taste of the metaphysical ideas of eighteenth- and nineteenth-century philosophers—ideas that were going out of fashion in standard American education. I learned about problems of consciousness and reality, conceptions of time and space, and so on. He was, at the time, much interested in Henri Bergson's ideas, and taught me to read Schopenhauer and Nietzsche. He also taught me the principles of experimental science, acquainting me with the works of thinkers like Francis Bacon and Darwin, and painstakingly describing methods of scientific research. He took me to the Academy of Sciences, where he finally held a decent clerical position, and let me go through the collections, identifying specimens of insects, birds, and mammals. He brought me many books on evolution, paleontology, and so on. He gave me my first ideas of political history, helping me through books by writers like Carlyle, Gibbon, Spencer, and Locke. He had been trained as a lawyer, and he discussed with me the principles of law. I even got a slight acquaintance with Blackstone, and learned to distinguish felonies from misdemeanors. My father had a type of mind that has, unfortunately, gone out of fashion today—the conceptual mind, which can take great pleasure in abstract speculation for its own sake. He was also an enlightened liberal political thinker who deplored narrow nationalism and prejudice of any sort. He had idealistic conceptions of justice and the basic equality of men, and was inclined toward socialism in a rather gentle way. Though he submitted to my mother in everything, he chuckled with me privately over Schopenhauer's "Essay on Women." Under his influence, I began to develop the scholarly sort of mind that I still possess. And I admired this intellectual attitude of his immensely. Unconsciously I think I must have tended to take his part against my mother. At any rate, scholarship and philosophy were subjects he and I had in common, subjects that my mother had no understanding of, or capacity for. I threw myself into this kind of learning as a sort of bastion against my mother's dominance, and I found that I had a much greater natural inclination toward it than I did toward the things my mother valued so highly—violin playing, for instance. The world of the intellect seemed to me a man's world.

In accepting my father's intellectual attitudes I became his friend and also his ally. There were always, somewhere in the picture, more dominating and aggressive men who were apt to get the best of him, and I wished to protect him against them. Since I was an extremely unaggressive person myself, however, most of my resentments in this connection were suppressed and produced anxiety rather than action. My uncle (my mother's brother, the surgeon) for a time assumed, in my mind, the position of my father's opponent, though outwardly we were very friendly with his family and respected him a great deal. To begin with, he was well off and very successful in his profession. When we visited his home we were distinctly in the position of poor relations. He was a man of considerable presence and dignity who exuded an atmosphere of authority. He was a kindly man also, and had, throughout his life, retained a great affection for our family. But he was a powerful man in the social sense—outwardly sure of himself, proud of his eminence, conservative in his political ideas, and anything but passive in his relationships. He was the sort of man whose jokes you laughed at as you would laugh at the jokes of royalty, out of an instinctive sense of obligation. He would not, however, respond similarly to your jokes. He would analyze them gravely to determine whether he really thought they were funny, and then either smile or decide that they were not worth smiling at. This attitude, with its implications of rejection, could at times be humiliating. Though he was a very able and successful surgeon and a prodigious scholar of natural science (particularly the flora, fauna, and geology of the Pacific Coast), he was lacking in the social elegance, agility of mind, and humor that my father possessed. But my father was always at a disadvantage when pitted against my uncle's more successful and aggressive personality, and I felt this disadvantage keenly. I wanted my father to shine in competition with my uncle, and this he could not do. There was always a slight element of condescension in my uncle's attitude toward him, and my father himself sometimes resented it, but, as usual, he was unable to retaliate.

My uncle was a realist and a man of common sense; my father was essentially a poet and an abstract thinker—and their ideas often conflicted, always to the public disadvantage of my father. My uncle was a scientist and an uninhibited progressive. He considered metaphysics, aesthetics, and philosophical speculation to be a waste of time, and he had no great feeling for poetry or fiction. He considered Nietzsche immoral (quite correctly), and wouldn't have his books in his house. (Having disposed of Nietzsche's thinking as immoral, he refused to demean himself to consider Nietzsche's point of view at all. My father also considered Nietzsche immoral, but that didn't keep him from a careful consideration of his ideas.) My uncle had heard that George Bernard Shaw had written a play (*The Doctor's Dilemma*) satirizing the medical profession. This was enough to cause him to ban the works of Shaw from his house. When my father mentioned certain of Shaw's works admiringly, my uncle would draw himself up with great dignity and change the subject. He had no sympathy with my father's gently socialistic ideas. He also considered many of my mother's notions—vegetarianism, nudism, and the terpsichorean training of male children—eccentric and ridiculous. He was an eminently sound man. He hated the Germans thoroughly during the First World War, and wouldn't have anything to do with Alfred Hertz, the conductor of the local symphony orchestra, because he was a German. My father, on the other hand, was at pains to defend the Germans as fellow humans throughout the war, I think mainly because he hated prejudice of any sort and considered our German friends to be underdogs during this period.

I admired my uncle greatly, but I also admired my father and resented my uncle's superiority of social rank. I became the champion of my father's ideas against my uncle's. I have even today a certain resentment against the smug and universally successful scientific mind, and I tend to defend the metaphysical, mystical, and aesthetic mind against it. Throughout the early part of my life I often got into hot, unreasonable arguments with materialists, and became extremely annoyed at their inability or unwillingness to consider the metaphysical point of view. I disliked the materialist for his sureness that he was right and for his lack of imaginative agility. I am sure that, in these arguments, I was unconsciously defending my father against my uncle; or perhaps sometimes against my mother or cousins (sons of my mother's brother), who, in this respect, I conceived to be in league against my father.

I have already described at length my idealistic love affair with Miss Nesbitt and its remarkable consequences to my career. I have, however, glossed over a lot of detail in the period from sixteen to twenty years old which occurred simultaneously with it. Let me now examine this period. It began roughly with my graduation from high school, extended through a year of concentrated musical study, and culminated in two years as a professional musician in San Francisco, after which my family took me to live in Europe.

Before I graduated from high school I had already determined to embark on a musical career. Since this ruled out going to college, it did not greatly matter whether I graduated or not. Miss Nesbitt had left San Francisco some time before, and my ties with school had become less close. My work on music, on the other hand, had become more absorbing. When I did graduate, I was under a cloud. I had had a row with my English teacher and had done poor work in this subject for the first time. (Oddly, English had been the subject I was best at.) The result was a technical delay in my graduation. I did not receive my diploma until several months following the regular exercises, and it was given me after I had made it plain that I had no intention of entering college. I wish, now, that I had gone to college—not primarily for the education (I am a far better educated man than most of the college men I know), but for the integration into social life that it would have offered me. Isolation from society had always been my curse. My musical career was to continue this isolation. I had finally been placed in the hands of a Polish violinist named Artur Argiewicz who was a far better violin teacher than my previous one had been. Now that I was free of school, I de-

voted all my energies to music, practicing the violin six hours
a day and working on musical composition three or four
more. I played in various amateur orchestras, participated in
chamber-music sessions with my brother and others, and, for
a time, conducted a student orchestra at the San Francisco
Conservatory of Music. Mr. Argiewicz, a Jew, had a rational
and intelligent attitude toward violin pedagogy. He was, in
fact, a man of superior intelligence in many ways. He treated
me as a fellow adult and succeeded in interesting me in the
violin as a problem in physiology and engineering. He had
been a pupil of Fritz Kreisler—Kreisler's only pupil, I believe.
He was assistant concertmaster of the San Francisco Symphony, and he trained me not only in the solo repertoire, but
in the orchestral repertoire as well, knowing that I had ambitions to become a conductor. Under him I worked very hard,
and by the time a year had passed, he got me an audition with
Alfred Hertz. I passed, and at the age of eighteen, became
the youngest member of the San Francisco Symphony, playing at the last desk of the second violins. It seemed to me a
great honor to play in the orchestra. I was an extremely conscientious violinist, and used the opportunity to study complete scores of the works we played. Meanwhile I continued
both my study of the violin and my study of musical composition, for I did not regard my career as being in any way
complete. This was only a stepping stone. Nevertheless I
found playing in the orchestra a thrilling experience, and it
redoubled my ambitions to be a symphony conductor. On the
whole, the other musicians accepted me cordially enough as a
comrade, though I shouldn't have blamed them if they
thought my tremendous ambitions a little pretentious. I did
not lead much of a social life with them outside rehearsals and
concerts. My ambitions were aimed at higher things, and I

was only eighteen, while they were all mature-to-aged men. Again I was cut off from social contact. I continued to live at home with my family, bringing home my weekly pay check and contributing to the family finances. Among my other studies I took up the piano again, and began to take lessons on the French horn, an instrument that has always been very congenial to me. I finally got to play the horn well enough to do some of the extra parts in the large symphonies. Meanwhile I managed a non-paying job as rehearsal pianist for the chorus in the San Francisco Opera. I had sung in the chorus of this opera company, and acted as supernumerary with the visiting Chicago and Scotti (or Metropolitan) opera companies. I now played in the orchestra of the San Francisco Opera as well as in the symphony. I was accumulating a considerable amount of general musical experience. But though I was becoming a fairly well rounded musician in some respects, I was not really a remarkable violinist outside the orchestra. I was still paralyzed with fear when I had to play as a soloist before people. And my mother still insisted that I scratched abominably while my brother played the cello beautifully. My brother did not play in the San Francisco Symphony. He continued, however, to be a much better cellist than I was a violinist. For all my theoretical musicianship and general knowledge, he outstripped me easily as a performer. He had given public recitals as a solo cellist from the age of ten, and was without the slightest trace of insecurity on the solo platform. He took a job for a while playing in the orchestra at a big German restaurant on Market Street, where he often appeared as soloist. I affected to look down on this sort of job, since the music he played was light in character. I was secretly aware, however, that it was harder to play as a soloist in the restaurant orchestra than as an anonymous second violinist in the symphony, and I think he was too. The family was already considering the idea of taking him to Paris to study for a career as a virtuoso. He was, without question, the most talented musician of the family. My greatest achievements continued to be in the academic and theoretical facets of the art, where a composer named Albert Elkus and a prodigious theoretician named Julius Gold were my teachers. Most of the theoretical training that I later found valuable, I absorbed from Gold's teaching. It went far beyond anything I was to learn later in Vienna.

By the age of nineteen, I was conducting a large orchestra at the Greek Theatre in Berkeley for the Greek tragedy performances of the actress Margaret Anglin, and this made me a public celebrity again for a short time. On this occasion I was not in the position of an exploited and half-baked infant prodigy. I knew something of the business of orchestra conducting. I had a complete understanding of rehearsing methods, cues, and so on, which I had learned by playing as a professional under the batons of others. I had an absolute confidence in my talents as a conductor, and I acquitted myself, I think, with remarkable competence. The episode was a tremendous boost for my ego. I conceived myself to be already a professional conductor who was whiling away his time playing in symphony orchestras awaiting a suitable opportunity to exercise his real talents. Doubtless it was only a question of time before the New York Philharmonic or the Metropolitan Opera would discover my abilities and offer me a job. It did not occur to me at the time that I had gotten this conducting job through the machinations of influential friends who knew Miss Anglin personally, and that Miss Anglin, with a sure theatrical instinct for publicity, had made the most of a situation involving a small-town prodigy conductor whose appearance in her productions might create local interest and bring in money at the box office. About five years later I approached Miss Anglin in New York thinking that she might use me as a conductor for some of her Broadway productions. I was a little humiliated to discover that Miss Anglin was not interested in hiring me in New York. There, I was merely one of many adult conductors of greater or lesser gifts, and had very little of a professional record to support my aspirations. The drama of the local boy making good no longer had any publicity value in these surroundings. New York is a metropolis, and a tough town for all but the most indomitable ambitions. And to cope with its musical life successfully one needs more than talent—one needs some sophistication and a knowledge of the ways of the world.

During the eighteen-to-twenty period, my social life, as I have explained, remained severely restricted. I lived with my family, worked feverishly at music, played in the symphony orchestra, and brought home my pay check. My ambitions left me no time for frivolities. I occasionally attended a movie with the family, but this was infrequent. I sometimes attended a party at my cousins' house, or went sailing with them on San Francisco Bay. I sometimes met and talked with artists, musicians, and architects who were friends of my parents, and who visited us now and then with their families. But I always felt that they were friends of my parents rather than friends of mine, and my relations with them were consequently constrained. After all, they were acquaintances of my mother, and they were interested in me only because I was her son. I could not move in these surroundings with any feeling of equality. Here and there I picked up casual acquaintances of my own, but they never seemed to develop into real friendships. My old high school friends had moved completely outside my orbit and were either at work or going to college. The men with whom I worked in the orchestra were all much older than I. The only contacts that I felt were truly my own were made in connection with some of my extracurricular musical activities. I conducted a little amateur orchestra in Sausalito for a while, and there I met a young writer named Whit Burnett who was an amateur viola player. We struck up a friendship which lasted, off and on, for many years, and it was partly through his interest and influence that I eventually turned to writing as a career. But my meetings with him were almost clandestine. I didn't like bringing him home with me. My mother was somewhat critical of him, and, besides, I didn't like my friends to meet my mother—I was afraid they would end up by liking her and rejecting me. Secretly I greatly admired my writer friend. He was a bohemian and a newspaperman. He knew something about the world, and discussed things like sex freely. He moved in a masculine cosmos, with no family to inhibit his actions. He was also somewhat older than I. But I never dared enter his cosmos to take part in its doings, though I was frequently invited to do so. I was afraid that the bohemia of San Francisco's writers and journalists would distract me from my career. And back of that career there was still the shadow of Miss Nesbitt urging me on to incredible feats. I envied my friend his world of realism, literary endeavor, newspapers, drink, and free love. But these things were a closed area for me as long as I clung to the idea of Miss Nesbitt and my necessity to be the greatest conductor in the world. Today I wish seriously that I had broken my chains and embarked then and there on a career of newspaper work. I even wish that I had entered on a couple of years of debauchery and reckless living. But my ego, twisted by my fear of the world, was too powerful for me to allow myself to do anything improper or unidealistic. I continued working at my career in my self-created prison. Already, however, I had begun to visualize the life of a writer as a free, masculine, and adventurous pursuit, in which one could, with courage, face the real world on its own terms. Writing, with its interest in people, sex, economics, and other realistic aspects of life, appeared to me, at the moment, to be a much more vulgar profession than music, with its world of aesthetic niceties. Writing also represented the realm of impulse and desire which I described at the beginning of this document as the world Mephistopheles introduced me to. At the time, this world seemed frightening, uncertain, and possibly evil to me. I was not ready to enter it. But my early experiences with my father and with my journalist friend were factors that led me to choose writing as a career later when my musical ambitions collapsed. Even today, I have a feeling that music exists in an artificial realm which I have found untrustworthy and, hence, have abandoned. My hold on the world of writing, on the other hand, has always seemed to me somewhat precarious. I have never been certain enough of my writing ability to embark on elaborate ventures in the purely literary field. I have tended to compromise, writing on subjects related to music, where I felt my knowledge to be on certain ground. Only very recently have I had the courage to launch myself on a career of political, humorous, and other general writing. And my articles of this type have been published in magazines where I had previously established my position as a writer on music. When, however, I undertook a job as music critic of *The New Yorker* later on, it seemed, somehow, that my gains as a writer on other subjects had been lost. Here I was, back again, concerned with the art that had betrayed me. The situation contributed to the nervous breakdown I described at the beginning of this narrative.

Despite my rather attenuated idealistic attachment to Miss Nesbitt—or to her mental image—I did drift into several quasi affairs with other girls. They all lacked stability because of my hopelessly exaggerated fidelity to her, and none of them eventuated in physical consummation. I remember thinking at the time how much at ease with women I had become because of my devotion to the absent Miss Nesbitt. The feeling of ease came, of course, from the conviction that I was absolutely independent of them, since my whole feeling of dependence, where women were concerned, now centered on Miss Nesbitt. Thus I could approach them in a carefree manner, noting that they attracted me and that I attracted them. I could even indulge in mild gestures of affection toward them without feeling that I was in the least involved. But actual sex intercourse was, of course, out of the question, since that would constitute a betrayal of the woman on whom I thought myself dependent. It will be noted here how thoroughly the female image represented by Miss Nesbitt had taken over the anchoring and inhibiting position originally occupied by my mother. Nevertheless I was disturbed by my growing sexual impulses. For a time I taught music twice a week at a country high school in Marin County, and I had several very attractive girls in my classes. I was, however, too timid about endangering my responsibilities as a teacher, to attempt any love-making here. At the San Francisco Conservatory of Music, where I also taught, I became acquainted with two or three girls with whom, at different times, I pursued relationships that were pleasant enough, though they never got beyond the "petting" stage. Girls who were friends of my family were absolutely taboo. My mother knew them, and therefore they were potentially in league with her against my masculinity. Toward the end of the sixteen-to-twenty period (that is, when I was about nineteen), there were two girls who nearly succeeded in dethroning Miss Nesbitt temporarily. The first of these was an actress whose name I have forgotten but who was the ingenue of Margaret Anglin's company when I was conductor of her orchestra. I fell in love with this young actress hook, line, and sinker, and carried on a rather moony relationship for several weeks. She, however, was older than I, and engaged to be married to somebody in New York, and she would have none of me. When I became somewhat aggressive, she fought with me and threw me out of her life entirely. I remember being so depressed over her rejection that I felt no worries at all while conducting Miss Anglin's orchestra. My heart was so thoroughly broken that I just didn't care whether I performed successfully or not. She soon left town, and I soon recovered.

The second of these girls was a hearty, healthy, and quite beautiful, though not very well educated, Irish girl named Wilma. I have forgotten how I met her. I think it must have been at a dance or some such affair that I attended. I introduced her to my cousins, and we sometimes went sailing together. I also took some hiking trips alone with her, and on one of them she offered herself to me. I didn't respond, though I wanted to. I pretended not to notice her advances. What an incredible prude I must have been! Wilma, however, became the prototype of another variety of woman with whom I fell in love in later life—the vital physical woman from the wrong side of the railroad tracks, the woman my mother and my romantic self would both have disapproved of. My most satisfying physical relationships have always been with such women, and these women have never coincided with the idealized type that moved me to dreams of power. Later in life I found myself a habitual bigamist who desired one woman for emotional dependence and another for sex. I never seemed able to combine the first function with the second in a single woman. Wilma was the first woman I ever knew who belonged to the second category. My relationship with her was frankly sexual, though it remained unconsummated. It was a simple physical attraction uncomplicated by consideration of brains or career, and I remember it with pleasure.

I remember just one other important incident related to sex from this period, and I adduce it to illustrate my mother's attitude. With my family I was visiting a small summer resort where I met a very pretty girl. As usual, I was attracted on sight. She asked me to come to a public dance one evening, saying that she was going to be there. She had a number of male admirers besides me, and I think my mother got wind of the situation and imagined that the girl was toying with my emotions. At any rate my mother insisted on accompanying me to the dance and dancing with me there, to my enormous humiliation. I was already about eighteen years old, and would willingly have accepted any emotional rebuff the girl had dealt me. This overprotective act on the part of my mother was one of the bitterest experiences of my life. Again, she had succeeded in depriving me from asserting myself as a man.

No attachment from this period succeeded in reaching any state of stability, however, for, shortly after my twentieth birthday, I was removed from my environment and taken to Europe. There, as I have already related, I met Miss Nesbitt again, and laid that ghost forever. I was by this time bound and determined at any cost to get away from my family, for I had found that living with them at the age of twenty simply involved one unbearable humiliation after another. I finally made my break, shortly after arriving in Paris, and left by myself for Vienna to undertake my musical studies there in solitude. Here began a different phase of my life—not a happier one, but at least one that was free of the influence of my mother. I now, somewhat hesitantly and unsuccessfully, tried to take over the job of converting myself into an adult.

In this process my hostility toward my mother and family became more or less overt, and it has continued so for the remainder of my life. I wrote my family letters from Vienna attempting to explain my attitude, and telling them that I had, for emotional reasons, to cut myself free of them. They were hurt by these letters, and failed utterly to understand me. A year or so later I returned to Paris, but I did not live with them any longer. My attitude toward them had now become more aggressive. I accused my mother of trying to tyrannize over me, and did my best to rescue my brothers from what I thought would be a similar fate. For several years I carried on a deliberate campaign to break up the ties that united the family. I became very bitter over my mother's early ideas about keeping the family together forever as a cooperative unit in which we would all live side by side and contribute our earnings to a common fund. I took every opportunity to emphasize my independence, and frequently ridiculed and condemned my mother's most cherished ideas about feminism, vegetarianism, sexual morality, and family solidarity. I encouraged my brothers to revolt against her too, feeling vaguely that she might be turning them into homosexuals or into neurotics like myself. From my own point of view this revolt was, of course, justified. But my parents never understood it. They felt that they had brought their children up admirably, and pointed proudly to our remarkable accomplishments and to the great sacrifices they had made to bring them about. I learned then that there is no use trying to explain the problems that arise between one generation and another.* My mother, in particular, was deeply hurt, and accused me of trying to "throw her out" of my life, which, of course, was precisely what I was doing. For many years I remained estranged from her, and approached her only in an armed state of polite hostility. In later life I seldom saw her. I took up residence in a different city and hoped fervently that she would never visit me. When she did, occasionally, I accepted her as politely as I could, but regarded the occurrence like a visitation of the plague, hoping desperately that she would soon go away again. I seldom corresponded with her. I carefully guarded her from meeting my friends, hated her to associate with my wife, and shied away from any intimacy with her acquaintances. Even today I seldom write her a letter, and communicate with her only once in every couple of years. I have a slight sense of duty toward her. If she were very ill, for example, I would feel bound to see that she was taken care of. But I would do this purely from a sense of moral obligation. I have, consciously, no feeling of affection toward her whatever. I do not know whether this complete estrangement of mine was emulated by my two brothers, or whether their lives were disturbed, as mine was, by my mother's influence. Both of them seem to have developed into successful men—I use the word successful in its psychological meaning: successful as personalities—though they, like me, have gone through numerous marriages. Only one has remained a musician, and he is the very talented cellist. The other has shown a preference for foreign wives—first a Russian girl, then a French one. The cellist—my immediate sibling rival as a child—lost his hostility

---

* The point I am writing about here has, as this goes to publication, been formalized and accepted as the "generation gap." It was not accepted then, but it existed all the same.

(or was it merely his need for attention) as soon as he passed adolescence, and our relations have been excellent for more than twenty-five years. We live, however, in three different cities, and seldom correspond.

In Vienna, where I took up the study of musical composition and attempted to improve my piano playing, I tended, as usual, to isolate myself. For several months I never spoke to a human being except my landlady and my teachers, and I communicated with them only as much as practical considerations forced me to. I was deeply unhappy, but I took out all my unhappiness in devotion to my work, studying hard all day, taking walks in the afternoon by myself, and broadening my knowledge of music by attending the opera and various concerts in the evening. Curiously, it never occurred to me that these concerts and opera performances were happy social affairs, and that most of the people who attended them got pleasure from the camaraderie of the occasion as well as from the music. I shied away from such social contacts. Occasionally I would meet someone at a concert and be invited out, but I never accepted these invitations. I regarded the whole art of music as a means to power and further isolation. I studied its technique like a dedicated madman, feeling that each new accomplishment would bring me nearer to my goal as a great conductor. I met several eminent musicians—among them Wilhelm Furtwängler and Pietro Mascagni. They were friendly to me, but I did not accept their friendship. I felt hopelessly inferior to them and would tremble and stutter in their presence. I felt that I could not possibly be accepted by them until I had reached such eminence that I could consider myself their equal. Instead of accepting their kindly overtures and profiting by their advice, I avoided them and went back to my lonely room, where I practiced like mad in the hope that someday I might equal them with astonishing feats as an artist.

I noticed many pretty girls in Vienna and used to follow them around the city in a desultory way. But I seldom spoke to any of them, and even if they were friendly I tended to avoid contact with them. I was afraid of rejection. Only one thing could redeem me from my hopeless feeling of inferiority, and that was to astonish them with my ultimate eminence as a musician. I was, of course, living on a very small budget as an impoverished student, and this, too, tended to reinforce my isolation. I could not afford to dress well or to take girls out. But this was only a minor factor. There were plenty of girls who would have been available even to one of my modest financial resources. If I had had any sense, I would have entered one of the large conservatories in Vienna and mingled in the rich and joyful student life that existed there. But this involved the possibility of competition and the fear of rejection. I avoided other music students. I studied privately with an old professor of composition and a young student teacher of the piano. I was more isolated than ever. My only friends during this period were a family of warm-hearted and impoverished Russian refugees who lived upstairs in the old rooming house where I lived in the suburb of Hietzing. They occasionally asked me to meals with them, though they were so poor they had scarcely anything to eat. One of these Russians, an older woman named Frau Kardaschoff, took a great fancy to me in a maternal way. She twitted me about my solitude and attempted to introduce me to a couple of girls who lived in the neighborhood. But the girls didn't appeal to me and I failed to respond. It was Frau Kardaschoff's considered opinion that I was too sweet and vulnerable to get along in the world. I am afraid she was about right.

During this period I developed a lifelong habit of substituting an interest in objects for an interest in people. I walked in lonely isolation all over Vienna, and knew every street corner and architectural quirk by heart. I developed a love for the atmosphere and personality of cities which remained with me for years. I knew the old palaces and museums thoroughly, and had a great affection for visual impressions—the cafés on the Ringstrasse, the little beer gardens with hedges around them, the outlying suburban towns ringed by the Danube and the hills of the Vienna Woods. But I saw all these things as they might have been seen by a disembodied spirit wandering in complete isolation from the human race. I never made contact with the human beings in the landscape. I loved the landscape itself, but it was to me a dead thing—safely dead in fact: It could offer me no competition; it had no power to reject me. I was, and remained, the perpetual outsider.

Into this dismal situation stepped the girl who was my first sexual companion and who ultimately became my first wife. It was characteristic that the act of breaking my isolation was performed by her, not me. I had been attracted distantly by many a girl in Vienna, but I had never made a move toward any of them. Ellen Appleton, as my future wife was named, intruded, so to speak, into my monklike existence. Her parents were old friends of my family, but I had not seen her since I was a child. My mother had once suggested that she would be a nice girl for me to marry, since her parents had a lot of money. She was now traveling in Europe, and decided to come to Vienna to visit me. I have no idea whether her parents and mine had connived at this eventuality. It may have been so. At any rate, she arrived. I arranged temporary living quarters for her nearby, and met her at the train. Ellen was not my idea of a pretty girl. Her nose was on the aquiline side. Her figure was short and slightly plump. There was something that seemed to me somewhat spinsterish about her mouth, and she had rather heavy legs. The only thing that was handsome about her was her hair, which was chestnut colored, rather long, and naturally wavy. But she made up somewhat for her physical shortcomings by an air of great health and vitality, an assertive manner, and considerable taste and expenditure in the way she dressed. She was a woman of wealth, which, to my impoverished self, meant a being from a strange, glamorous world. She had the air of independence and self-assurance that goes with money, and she was traveling alone in Europe with a magnificence and a show of worldly experience that I found both impressive and somewhat enviable. She spoke no German, but she spoke both French and Italian with fluency and ease. She had been studying singing in France and Italy, and though I could perceive from the first note she sang for me that she had no talent whatever, she had a rather mild and casual ambition to be an opera singer. She was a nice girl; she seemed to like me and to have great admiration for my musical skills. We obviously had certain interests in common, and had known each other in childhood. Considering the self-imposed limitations of my lonely cosmos, she was the only available woman, for, though I had seen many women who attracted me more, I was cut off from them by my inability to make any move toward human contacts. So it was natural that I should drift into an affair with her. At first it was not a physical affair. I was, as usual, the courtly lover. I showed her around Vienna. We went to the opera together. I found that, having a companion, I had a new means of coping with social problems. She was rather aggressive in society, and I was glad to tag along, with her as my protector. I was, of course, drifting toward a sort of mother-son relationship in which I occupied a passive and submissive position.

She moved with ease in areas which frightened me. In some ways we reversed the normal masculine-feminine relationship. I provided the taste, the sensitivity, the poetic and aesthetic sensibilities, the submission, and the need for protection; she supplied the assertiveness and protectiveness that are usually the province of the male. Years later I learned that she had developed into a lesbian. There was very little in the way of a romantic atmosphere about this affair. It was very different from the passionate, idealized, and heroic theatricality that Miss Nesbitt had inspired. I evidently felt, in my loneliness, that I needed a woman to protect me. She willingly undertook the task. Before she left Vienna, after a visit of three weeks or so, I had asked her to marry me and she had accepted. She was henceforth known as my "fiancée." Again I had rushed into a trap, deliberately assuming obligations where a woman was concerned. I assumed them in return for protection from the world. My instinct was still to isolate myself— now with her as the protector of my isolation. After she left, I continued my lonely existence, studying hard and corresponding with her regularly. By the following summer I was visiting her in Italy, where she lived in a fashionable *pensione* in Florence.

There, she introduced me to a number of people—fellow students, Italian aristocrats, and members of the international colony. Under her protection I began to lead something in the way of a social life. But I never went out without her, or had the enterprise to make any contacts except those she made for me. I absorbed a great deal of sight-seeing with her. I became well acquainted with the art and architecture of a good part of Italy. We traveled together, and on one of our journeys, in Venice, we had our first sexual experiences. For me, it was about time, and I found the act, at first, very gratifying. I probably felt unconsciously that I would have preferred a companion who attracted me more passionately. But, after all, she was my "fiancée." Sexual relations with anybody else would have been unthinkable. I was never, throughout my relationship with Ellen, in love with her. But she became the center of a whole constellation of needs—for dependence, for companionship, for stability, and for protection from social hazards. She was also sufficiently attractive to me physically to provide a quenching effect on my youthful sexual urges. It will be seen, from the tone in which I write, that I was disappointed and frustrated, that I desired other women more than her, and that I had probably made a very unwise step. But that was how I made my bed, and for several years I was to lie in it, and even to pretend to others and to myself that I liked it that way. One of the deepest characteristics of a true neurotic is that he is capable of sincerity neither toward others nor toward himself.

It is obvious from what I have just written that the relation which I bore to Ellen was not a normal sexual one. I was following an old childhood pattern. As a male, I was not asserting myself much more successfully than I had against my mother. I had merely dropped my real mother and acquired a substitute for her. The substitution was, of course, not exact. Ellen was a young girl, and the possession of a "fiancée" gave me, from the outward social point of view, the appearance of a man who had fulfilled himself by acquiring a mate. This appearance, however, was deceptive. On the surface it gratified me, as I seemed to be carrying out a social ceremony that was associated with maturity. Actually, however, the whole ceremony was an act, concealing a relationship that never got beyond the infantile stage. I was still a frightened little boy, desperately seeking a woman on whom I could depend. And my hunger for masculinity was completely frustrated by the conflicting hunger for dependence. This pattern, and the conflict which it represented, was to pursue me throughout most of my adult life, forcing an element of frustration into nearly all my relations with women. It was the root of my later division of all women into women who were friendly (i.e., women on whom I could depend) and women who were sexually attractive (i.e., women with whom I could assert myself as a male). I desperately needed both the dependence and the assertion. But I never seemed able to find both of the necessary elements in a single female. I found the sexually attractive woman impossible to live with, and the mother substitute impossible to sustain a sexual interest in. Any prolonged association with the latter eventuated in impotence, desire for outside sexual gratification, and, finally, an intolerable feeling of confinement from which I had to break just as I had broken with my real mother.

After a period of living and studying in Italy and Vienna, we moved to Paris. We were now living unabashedly as man and wife. We occupied quarters in a little left-bank hotel, sufficiently far away from my family to be free of casual and unexpected visits. Occasionally I dropped in to see them, but I always took Ellen with me as a sort of buffer to protect myself against them. Again, with Ellen as my sole companion, I devoted myself assiduously to my musical studies, concentrating mainly on the violin and developing a proficiency at it that I had never before approached. Though Ellen made some social contacts, I tended to remain aloof. I met few of the colony of American expatriates who had, at that time, converted Paris into a capital of American culture. I associated almost exclusively with my music teachers, moving among the colorful throngs of Paris with that same disembodied air of

isolation that I had shown in Vienna. The writer friend whom
I had cultivated in San Francisco appeared in Paris, came to
see me, and soon was taking an active part in the literary
scene. Prohibition, war memories, and the astringent face of
President Coolidge had made Paris the center of the American
intellectual scene, and the city was certainly a center of cos-
mopolitan culture. Joyce, Gertrude Stein, Hemingway,
Pound, Henry Miller, and many others were there. He knew
them all. I didn't. I practiced my fiddle in solitude. I saw him
occasionally, but I never developed any great intimacy with
him or with his friends. And I never went near Fontainebleau,
where the American Academy under Nadia Boulanger was
turning out American composers, either. I didn't much like
the music that was issuing from Fontainebleau. I had done
my studies in composition in Vienna where there still remained a vestige of the grand Central European tradition, and
where standards of musical performance were far higher than
those in Paris. I was lonely, but I think musicians are likely
to be lonely. Their craft demands years of solitary labor. Few
people except other musicians have any understanding of their
art—least of all literary men (despite one or two outstanding
exceptions like George Bernard Shaw). When "the arts" are
put together for some generalization, or other purpose, it is
likely that the art of music will be completely misunderstood.
Its practitioners work in a closed environment, cut off from
communication with other artists. Even painters—who are always trying to imitate the aesthetic peculiarities of music and
imagine it to be "abstract"—do not understand it. As a rule,
they prefer music-hall tunes to symphonies. At the time,
painting was the art that dominated Paris, with literature
coming in a close second. Most of the music being fostered
there represented a curious art—really the art of painting

transmuted into sound. I had avoided Paris purposely as a place to study composition. I studied the violin there, with a master pedagogue named Lucien Capet.

I came to know Paris well, in my curious, detached way, but I knew it, as I had known Vienna, and Italy, as a landscape full of inanimate objects and people with whom I had no contact. Such small contacts as I had were provided for me by Ellen. After a little over a year of this life, I discovered that the conductor Walter Damrosch was in Paris, and asked him for an audition. I played the violin and the French horn for him and showed him some of my compositions. I was rewarded with a contract to play second violin in the New York Symphony the following season, and I considered this an important step toward my future career. That summer we moved to New York, where Ellen's family lived. I had never been in New York before, and I found it a rather rough, overwhelming, alien city after my long stay in Europe. But I had Ellen to protect me, and her family, with whom I lived for a few months, seemed to like me. I had a job, and things seemed to be looking up.

Late that summer, while living with Ellen's family, I evidently sensed a necessity to do something on my own. I went off by myself to Stamford, Connecticut, in search of a vacation at the seashore. I rented a small, furnished room not too far from the beach, and went swimming every day. I stayed there about two weeks, and they were miserable weeks. I seemed unable to strike up an acquaintance with anybody. I ate in cheap restaurants, and spent my time either swimming by myself or wandering disconsolately around the town. Here there were no beautiful objects of architecture to attract me. I found Stamford incredibly drab after Europe. I was glad to get back from my vacation, and I now took up quarters in a

furnished room in Greenwich Village. I had arranged it so
that Ellen could visit me there. Several notable incidents took
place during this period. Previous to my lone trip to Stamford
(and perhaps the cause of it) was a bad situation that developed between me and my prospective in-laws. Ellen became pregnant and unwisely confessed her condition to her
mother, thinking that we could get married immediately, and
that there was nothing to worry about. Her mother was sympathetic, but promptly put the whole problem up to Ellen's
father, who was infuriated. It had evidently never crossed his
mind that his daughter and I had been living in sin, and he
was a man with a crushing sense of propriety. Any idea of
marriage followed by a childbirth a month or so too soon was
apparently an intolerable humiliation to him. He took me
aside for a bitter lecture in which he seriously suggested that
the proper penalty for my crime should be castration. In fact,
he brought up a parallel with Heloise and Abelard. Ellen's
mother threatened to have a heart attack unless something
were done. I didn't take the father's threats very seriously
myself, but the whole situation did worry me because of
Ellen. I myself didn't see why we couldn't get married and
forget about the supposedly criminal aspects of the case. But
the father was adamant. He was a physician. He insisted on
performing an abortion personally on his daughter. I dared
not interfere, since Ellen was unwilling to hurt her father by
refusing to submit, though we both would liked to have had
the child. So old man Appleton went through with his rather
primitive plan. (He felt that his social position was jeopard-
ized. Perhaps it was.) When it was all over, Ellen and I decided to get married, and the following winter our wedding
was held at her home. But relations between me and her father
remained strained forever after. It might be concluded that

this experience was a great shock to me. Actually I don't think it was. For all my conventionality about being faithful to a woman, I was quite unconventional about the formalities of marriage—and so was Ellen. We both considered the old man to be dead wrong, but we had to placate him. As a matter of fact, Ellen had had an abortion before, in Italy, and though it had worried us considerably at the time, she had gone through with it without very much trouble. Perhaps unconsciously, in view of my mother's early lectures about woman's suffering through sex (childbirth), these incidents affected me more than I realized. But on the surface at least there were no overwhelming feelings of guilt, just the rational worry and regret for pain inflicted that the average normal human being would feel. Of course, the idea that I had caused all this suffering to Ellen did tend to increase my sense of obligation toward her. But she herself seemed resilient, good-humored, and ready to take on any pain or trouble that fate inflicted on her. The marriage seemed an appropriate gesture of appeasement on my part. After causing all this difficulty, the least I could do was marry her. We had intended to get married anyhow. If anyone ever reads these lines, he will probably be struck by an atmosphere of cold-bloodedness that permeates them. There is no warmth in what I have written about Ellen; no human sympathy. I have already stated that I was never in love with her. I maintained, throughout this episode, my customary passivity. As usual, I was lacking in any strong emotion except fear. I wanted very much to do the right thing, to make amends, to fulfill my obligations and perform what I had promised to perform. Actually I was acting against my will, but my capacity for enterprise had struck such a low ebb that I had no idea what my will was. I was, foolishly enough, submitting to everybody—to Ellen, to her parents, to my own infantile conceptions and fears. It is easy to speculate on alternatives: If I had been in love with the girl I should have defied her parents and run away with her; if I was not in love with her I should simply have walked out and made a life for myself somewhere else. But, not being in love, I hadn't the strength to do the former, and being the kind of infantile neurotic I was, I was afraid to do the latter. Typically, dependence won out, and I chose to cling to the woman at any cost. Typically, later, I found this dependence an unendurable trap and had to escape it at any cost. But this situation belongs a little later in my narrative.

So, for a number of reasons, none of which was the right one, I became a married man. I can remember a strong feeling of resentment at the wedding ceremony itself. I disliked the minister and the air of slightly smug respectability and wealth that surrounds the Episcopal Church, which he represented (and which my parents had once belonged to). I disliked my father-in-law for what seemed to me his hypocrisy in ceremoniously giving away his daughter after having deprived her of her pregnancy. I also disliked, and still dislike, the sort of man he was—unctuous, ambitious to move among people of wealth and social standing, a stickler for propriety but, I am sure, a person capable of the shadiest ethics in his profession if he stood to gain by them, a snob filled with the particular sort of snobbery that characterizes the humbly born social climber, and a figure who had reached such eminence as he had attained by connivery and connections rather than by any conspicuous ability in the noble craft of medicine. He

was, I suppose, a typical "society doctor." He had come into
his money by ingratiating himself with a very wealthy woman,
whose idiot son had been his patient. After the death of her
son, she had legally adopted him and his family, making them
her heirs provided they remained her companions until death.
She was a crotchety and demanding old woman. Their life
with her was affluent, filled with travel, elegant limousines
with chauffeurs, country and city homes, and so on. But they
had to be good to their benefactress and cater to her slightest
whims. In reality, they were waiting for her to die, and secretly they were impatient about it, dreaming of a future of
freedom and wealth based on the old woman's legacy. Fitted
into this picture, my father-in-law's anxiety over a hasty marriage and premature birth was somewhat logical. Everything
depended on keeping up the appearance of virtue so as not
to scandalize the old lady. But the picture was not a pretty
one. I myself, having been brought up without any particular
respect for wealth and a great respect for achievement, regarded it with concealed contempt. The contempt was concealed because I was afraid to express it lest it interfere with
my sense of emotional security, since, emotionally, I was
entirely dependent on Ellen. Several times my father-in-law
offered to lend me money. I never accepted his offers. I was
anxious to make my own way, and I had a horror of being
entrapped in the financial and social machinations of the Appleton family.

Meanwhile I continued to play the violin in the New York
Symphony. My distaste for the profession of an orchestra
player projected itself on my colleagues to the point where
I regarded them as a bedraggled, clannish, and unintelligent
lot of peasant Europeans whose outlook and social habits resembled those of waiters or barbers rather than artists. They

were not, as a whole, as cultivated as the musicians of the San Francisco Symphony had been. Whatever glamour had surrounded playing in an orchestra soon evaporated. I could hold an intelligent conversation about music with very few of them. Many had minds that were limited to the discussion of technicalities about oboe reeds or horn mouthpieces, or to such general subjects as where to find prostitutes, how to get extra jobs in theatres or hotels so as to make more money, or how to get back to the "old country," where life was easier if less remunerative. But I am painting an untrue picture. There were interesting men among these musicians, some able artists, and one or two men of notably generous character. Though many of them had come from societies of the monarchic type (this was not long after the First World War), they had come to America looking for freedom, only to find themselves cogs in that most monarchic of institutions, the symphony orchestra. Nearly all of them were Europeans; many could hardly speak English. I am aware that the make-up of symphony orchestras has changed drastically since that time, and that nowadays most symphonic musicians in America are Americans. I am also aware that today playing in a great symphony orchestra is a much more respected profession (and incidentally a much higher-paid one) than it was then. But this was in the mid to late nineteen twenties. As for me, I felt abandoned in a completely distasteful world with no clear idea how to get out of it, and I felt deeply cheated. This was not the life of achievement I had promised myself; it appeared to me to be a degrading artistic slum, inhabited by uninteresting people with whom I could find nothing in common. Except for Ellen, I was desperately alone. I could make no satisfactory contact with my colleagues, and yet, being one of them, I felt myself to be an outcast in the outer, commercial, world. It was becoming evident to me that musicians—or at least the sort of musicians I moved among —were not highly regarded in the social structure of New York, and, indeed, didn't deserve to be. We had the social status and mental orientation of servants. I was also aware that my prowess as a violinist would never be sufficient to raise me out of this milieu into the position of a concert soloist. I was still a very nervous violinist anyhow, and would never have dared to present myself as a solo concert artist. This, as I have already explained, was a result of my lifelong resentment against the violin. Moreover, it was becoming more and more obvious that my one important musical ambition—to transform myself into a symphony conductor—was surrounded with bewildering problems. One didn't rise out of the symphonic ranks to become a conductor. There were no established channels through which an American musician could rise to become a conductor. There were, in fact, no American conductors of any importance. The days when Leonard Bernstein made the American conductor not only a competent but a brilliant and glamorous figure had not arrived. When people wanted a conductor they imported a man of established reputation from Europe. Conceivably, with great effort, pulling social strings and making personal connections (which I was conspicuously inept at), I might have maneuvered myself into a position as conductor of a suburban chorus or a theatre orchestra. But this was too disappointing an objective. I had no desire to conduct popular music or amateur suburban choruses or orchestras. I wanted to conduct symphonies—to start at the top, and the top was simply not accessible to me. I knew hundreds of symphonic scores by heart. I was convinced of my talent, but the opportunity to exercise it was so far beyond my reach as to appear an utterly hopeless objective.

I was, I can see now, caught up in the desperate competitive struggle which had left many a hopeful musician by the way-side in the American musical scene. New York orchestras were full of would-be conductors. So were hotel ensembles, theatre pits, and burlesque houses. Few of them ever got anywhere. The best of them ended up as music teachers, operatic coaches, orchestral managers, or technicians of one sort or another in the movies or radio. For the artistically ambitious man the whole field of symphony orchestras seemed a cage with no exit. Actually though, it is true that a very few of my colleagues *did* manage to make the transition. The first of them was George Raudenbusch, a violinist in Damrosch's orchestra with whom I had often played string quartets, who became conductor of the Harrisburg Symphony. Later on, two members of the New York Philharmonic, where I worked under Toscanini, made it. They were Leon Barzin, who became conductor of the National Orchestral Association (a training orchestra) and of the Balanchine Ballet Company, and Alfred Wallenstein, who eventually became conductor of the Los Angeles Philharmonic and even the N.B.C. Symphony for a time. But none of these men seemed able to reach the top of the conducting profession—not, at least, what I considered to be the top. As for me, I failed even to make an effort. I think that I expected some flaming angel to descend suddenly to earth and proclaim me to be a rival of Toscanini. I had no friends in high places who could help me; I had hardly any friends of any kind. I had broken with the Appleton family, who were the only people of wealth and influence I had known in New York. I was, as usual, completely alone. And, beyond these considerations, I retained that curious incapacity to assert, or promote, myself in any way. The problem was similar to the one of not being able to run for class president in high school.

I could fight in behalf of others, but I could make not the slightest move to put myself forward. I suppose that if I had loved the art of music sufficiently for its own sake I might have eventually been content to saw away my life as a modest second fiddler. But I did not have that much love for music. I wanted prestige and power, and music as a means to these objectives was obviously the wrong career.

Being completely thwarted in my specific ambition, I strove for crumbs of prestige by branching out in my activities. Anxious to be anything but an orchestral violinist and horn player, I took jobs arranging music for theatrical performances, and composed a considerable amount of incidental music for ballets and other dance spectacles. I also taught musical composition. These activities were not particularly remunerative, but at least they offered me the opportunity to call myself something besides one of Walter Damrosch's second violinists. The world outside my orchestral profession seemed a very desirable place. It was full of glamorous women and glamorous occupations carried on by people who seemed happy and active. But I felt that it was a world that excluded me. The only thing I knew how to do for a living was play the fiddle, and I was not even a remarkably good fiddler. I attempted to act as though I regarded my profession as a dignified one. My appearance became very "musical." I wore striped trousers, a broad-brimmed black hat, and spats. I carried a cane and cultivated sideburns. I even spoke occasionally with a fake European accent. Actually this accent was not entirely unnatural. It enabled me to be better understood among my musical colleagues, few of whom knew English well. To most people I must have looked rather exotic—like a "typical" musician. Only the most psychologically acute among them would have guessed that this masquerade was an effort to impress a world that I thought had rejected me.

Occasionally, with my wife, I entered the non-musical world as exemplified in afternoon teas and evening affairs at the homes of various Manhattan bourgeois people. I was, however, extremely shy about making contact with them. I often sat for long periods without engaging in conversation. They conversed about things—politics, the theatre, the doings of artistically or socially prominent people—that I knew little about and did not dare venture opinions on. I hid behind my wife's skirts, so to speak, and hoped fervently that people would accept me as a shy, absent-minded, and rather poetic type of fellow—maybe a potential "genius." At the same time I loathed this public picture of myself. I wished to shine socially, to appear intelligent and urbane, and to assert myself in normal intercourse with average people. But I seldom dared even to enter an ordinary conversation for fear of exposing my ignorance of the world. Sometimes my hostess or some other person present would attempt to draw me out by pulling the conversation around to music. I would immediately be overcome with anger. The anger was because people thought me incapable of discussing anything except music. I took their efforts to discuss my profession as if they implied a humiliating condescension toward me. It was as if they had said: "This poor fellow is ill at ease because he is a complete nitwit about everything outside of music. We must help him by discussing what he knows." Unconsciously the term "musician" was beginning to assume in my mind the tone of rejection that the term "kike" means to a neurotic and overly race-conscious Jew. It was a term designating an outcast. Not until several years later did I give up music as a profession. The transition was necessarily gradual. At times I still managed to preserve the dwindling hope that I might somehow get to be a conductor, and I would often have dreams, and waking daydreams, in which I conducted symphony orchestras in my imagination, going through the baton movements in my mind and singing the music, which I knew by heart, to myself. For years the vision of myself stepping out onto the stage before a fine orchestra remained a heady and stimulating dream, seeming to offer me an illusory justification for what had been, otherwise, an unsatisfactory life. The dream died hard. Even ten years later, after I had long since given up any practical hope of conducting an important orchestra, the vision would persist, and, thinking of my years of musical study and my unexhibitable but substantial talent for orchestral conducting, I would be overcome with depression. Today I no longer have the slightest conscious desire to be a symphony conductor. The whole idea of polishing the details of routine, conventional symphonic music bores me, and I have achieved a compensating satisfaction in other lines of work. Nevertheless I still have frequent dreams in which I am about to conduct orchestras. Usually, in them, something happens to frustrate me from carrying out the task. My whole approach to the problem of a musical career had been as unrealistic as that of a child wishing to possess the moon. Even had I, by some barely conceivable stroke of luck, realized my dream, I should probably have been disappointed. The vague glamorous image of myself as a great conductor was as insubstantial and as far from reality as the glamorous image of Miss Nesbitt that had done so much to inspire it. It was, like her, a figment of my imagination, an unattainable illusion.

The death of the dream was, as I have said, a slow process. At the time I married, it was already beginning to die. Having saved up a little money by the end of my first season with the

New York Symphony, I took my newly married wife to San Francisco with me for a long summer vacation. I had always loved San Francisco. I disliked New York at that time, and I still possessed the restless illusion that one can get rid of one's troubles by changing the scene. We had lived in Paris like bohemians. We tried a similar life in San Francisco, living in a small apartment atop Telegraph Hill, doing our own cooking, and occasionally patronizing the Italian restaurants in the neighborhood. It soon became obvious, however, that a life of idleness in San Francisco's Latin Quarter was not the answer to the problems and frustrations that beset me. I went on practicing my fiddle and French horn, but I was conscious of a growing feeling of complete discouragement. Why was I practicing endlessly on the violin, which I hated and which was the badge of my humiliation and my frustrated career? I was actually practicing it through habit—because I had always practiced it, because it gave me something to do, because I was afraid that if I stopped I might lose my technique and with it my only method of earning a living. Meanwhile I started, in a desultory way, to study art. I attended life classes and drew from nude models. It seemed, at the time, somehow to fit in with my general artistic and bohemian way of life. At the art classes, I met women who appealed to me, but my sense of loyalty to, and dependence on, Ellen made it impossible for me to approach them. Meanwhile my sexual relations with Ellen became practically nonexistent. I found it impossible to look at her without a sense of horror. Little points about her physical appearance that I had always slightly disliked magnified themselves into deformities. I realized that I had never been in love with her. I felt hopelessly trapped in my marriage. Yet it was not she who had trapped me, but I who had trapped myself. The trap was my own helpless feeling of dependence on her. She was my protector and my only friend, my mother substitute. I was torn between my physical revulsion toward her and my desperate fear of being abandoned by her in a hostile world. I can see, in retrospect, that, although she did not fully understand my state, she acted with the utmost good will and patience. She even encouraged me to go out with other women, but I was so overwhelmed with a feeling of guilt toward her that I could not bear the idea of sexual relations with anyone else. I could not tolerate the idea of being an unfaithful husband, since I would, by being unfaithful, forfeit my right to dependence on her. I began seeking autoerotic sexual outlets, but this terrified me. It was obviously not a solution; it brought on intense attacks of depression; and was associated in my mind with guilt and self-mutilation. (I had never experienced the masturbatory activities that normally follow puberty, and, as an adult, such activities seemed unnatural and insane.) I began showing signs of invalidism. Fears of getting out of bed or of going anywhere by myself began to develop. I clung to my wife like a child clinging to its mother. I suppressed by main force my hostile impulses toward her. I could not bring myself in any way to approach the idea that I actually hated her—yet, obviously that was the case.

At about this time my money began to run out, and, being unwilling to borrow from her family, I tried a job playing the violin in a San Francisco movie house. I was not very experienced, however, in this sort of work, and I approached it with great nervousness, making a number of mistakes. It happened that the movie, that week, was a comedy, and periodically gales of laughter swept the theatre. I was convinced that the laughter was aimed at me for my ineptitude as a violinist. I left the job, shaking, after one performance. I was living in a world of supernatural horror. At home, I found that I could no longer even practice the violin. Again, I tried the vain hope of escape through change of scene. I moved with Ellen to a small cottage on the country place of some relatives, thinking that perhaps I was physically ill, and that the country air would do me good. But my troubles moved with me, and were even intensified by the lack of any occupation. I became practically unable to move. I lay in bed like an invalid. I contemplated suicide as the only possible way out, and then, paradoxically, became terrified that I would kill myself. Probably what I really wanted to do was to kill Ellen. But this I was too psychologically naïve to know. At any rate I became violently afraid of high places, sharp objects, such as knives, and anything else that offered the means to sudden death. Underneath all this murky horror I must have had some vague inkling of the causes of my trouble, for it ultimately became obvious to me that, if I were to survive, I must at any cost get away from Ellen. Finally in a state of desperation (I had been so harassed by fear that I hadn't eaten in days) I steeled myself to tell her that I had to leave her. The moment I made this assertive gesture toward her, I was swept by a wave of great affection for her coupled with a horrible sense of guilt over what I had done. I boarded a train for New York. She saw me off, and I never saw her again except fleetingly in the years that followed, always on terms of friendly formality.

On the train I paced the platforms most of the way, smoking endless quantities of cigarettes. I blamed myself unmercifully for what I had done. I seemed deliberately to have cut myself adrift from the only friend I had in the world. I was in the middle of a breakdown, suffering from alarming symptoms whose causes were almost entirely mysterious to me. And I was alone, severed from the only person I trusted. I did not particularly want to return to New York, but I had nowhere else to go, no friend whom I was really intimate with, no place to offer me refuge. One thing I knew. If I were not going to commit suicide, I must somehow continue the motions of living. In New York I had a job. I must manage to do that job, for on it depended my livelihood. It was no longer a question of ambition or career. It would be enough of a task merely to force myself to put one foot before the other and prove that I could fulfill the bare requirements of existence. I suffered daily from neurotic symptoms that have since become very familiar to me, fits of acute, almost unbearable, depression, fears that I would not be able to accomplish the simplest things, like eating or remaining seated in a chair or crossing a street, a terror of meeting people, and so on. I was convinced that I was partially insane, and it seemed desperately necessary to impersonate a sane man, so to speak—to force myself to go through normal motions, as if by doing so I could help convince myself that my mind was not completely unhinged. I dreaded every day. But I found that by taking myself in hand and forcing myself through every moment of the day, I could at least have the satisfaction of conquering my fears in continuous battle. It never occurred to me to consult a psychiatrist. I had no faith that any other human being could help me. I started a grim and determined fight to subdue my fear. The fight lasted in its acute form for about five years, relieved only occasionally by moments when depression was absent. I would not willingly relive those years. They were the closest thing to hell on earth that I can imagine.

The symptoms of this breakdown were exactly the same as those that appeared again at forty-five and caused me to seek psychiatric help. But my battle against them on this previous occasion was entirely my own. On two or three occasions, early in the battle, I attempted confiding my troubles to other people. I remember discussing the state of my mind with a woman who had been friendly with my wife, and later once or twice with certain of my musician colleagues. The result of each of these attempts to gain understanding and sympathy was a terrific increase in my depression. It was obvious that they didn't really understand what I was talking about, though they were sympathetic. There was also, I think, on my part, a desperate fear of becoming dependent on them as I had been on my wife. Evidently no one could help me but myself. I adopted the only method I could think of, which was essentially that of violent repression, though it resembled a sort of thought control such as that practiced by Christian Scientists. I treated my irrational fears as objects in themselves, to be abolished by efforts of the will. I found that I could sometimes be successful at this game. The logic of the method was about as follows: There was no sense in being miserable, since my misery was making life almost unbearable for me. Misery existed in the mind. Presumably I had control of my mind—or at any rate I could learn how to control it. Therefore all I had to do was to throw the misery out of my mind and I would be all right. I am now aware that this was a very primitive and ineffective substitute for psychiatry. Essentially it was an attempt to abolish the symptoms by a vigorous denial that they existed. It is, of course, practiced in daily life by many people, and is the average person's habitual way of dealing with small emotional upsets. It is the "feel-blue?-just-snap-out-of-it" theory of retaining mental balance, and is a perfectly good theory for normal people. The application of this theory to combat exacerbated neurosis, however, is apt to produce very dangerous and uncertain results, for it completely ignores the causes of the neurosis, and really does nothing toward eliminating them.

The mind then, presumably, could be controlled. One could think about whatever one wished to think about. So, think about something pleasant. This is not as easy as it sounds. What is pleasant? Trees and lawns and running brooks are pleasant. Let's think about them. The trouble is that one is merely thinking about the memory of certain sensual impressions. One's mind is not really occupied by them, and the nameless fear is still gnawing—still threatening total disaster. Try looking at pictures. Art is an interesting thing. But its subjects are apt to be frightening. Pictures of women produce anxiety because they stimulate sexual desire. Pictures of violence also produce anxiety. Pictures are apt to remind you of things you are trying to forget—people, landscapes, regions associated with your past—and you are trying to forget your past because it is filled with horror. You must, at any cost, crush that past. It is not a part of you. You are starting over again from scratch. Try looking at pictures the way painters and art critics do, studying them in terms of lines, textures, and other abstract features. That is a little better. Everything, to an artist, may be seen as lines, masses, and colors—elements in a visual composition. In a way, that simplifies life. It makes everything potentially beautiful. Even a shipwreck or a bombing can be reduced to elements of line and color. Maybe the world doesn't exist except as an impression on the retina. Maybe it is dead, and without power to harm me. There is a little comfort in this thought, but the gnawing animal within me still rages under the surface. I can't deceive myself. Things are not dead; they are real and changing. Change. That is one of the most terrifying things about life. One changes. One has to change whether one likes it or not. The gnawing animal wants me to change. Let me look in the mirror. Perhaps I do not look as insane as I feel. Well, I look rather pale and drawn;

not exactly a picture of blooming health. I seem to need a shave. Horrifying thought. Those whiskers keep on growing relentlessly. They will never stop. Like all the rest of me they are changing continuously. Into what? God knows. One must continue to shave every day. One does not stop. One must change. One moves continuously from the past into the future. One is not a dead aesthetic composition consisting of lines and colors. One is alive. If only one could arrest that life. No! One mustn't think that way. One must think pleasant thoughts. How hard it is! That razor could be used to slash one's wrists. Let us put it away out of sight. One mustn't think this way. But one *is* thinking this way. I must get my back against the wall. I must determine, no matter what, that I will not give in to the gnawing animal. I must beat it into submission no matter what effort this takes. Perhaps I ought to pray. Please God, let me find some way out of this. But I really have no faith in God. I must find a way out by myself. I am acting like a child. I must discipline myself. I must occupy my mind with something. One cannot simply stop thinking unpleasant thoughts. One must replace them by thinking actively about something else. Let us try practicing the violin. This is a sort of discipline. But it isn't discipline enough. One can still think, while moving one's fingers unconsciously through the music. If one could only stop thinking! If one could go to sleep and stay asleep permanently. But that would be death. Mustn't think about death. Think pleasant thoughts. Get a pencil and a piece of paper and start writing. Put your thoughts down on paper, the kind of thoughts you *must* think; pleasant, affirmative, creative thoughts. Keep thinking and writing. It is hard work. That is what you need. Train your mind to work hard, thinking and writing. Write every day. Try to figure life out and write about it. Set yourself a task and carry it through. When you are writing you can't think about anything else. As long as you are writing, the gnawing animal cannot destroy you, for you are controlling your mind. Write until your mind is exhausted. It will fill up the time until you can go to bed.

This is a picture of what happened daily during this period. I found in writing a means of displacing suicidal thoughts from my mind; and I began to write a great deal in a rather unsystematic way—notes on music and aesthetics, morals, and other subjects. I was, however, unable to write about my personal troubles, for my whole method of dealing with them lay in hiding them from myself. I was deathly afraid to look into the processes of my own mind. I was afraid of finding insanity there. I was building a solid wall between myself and the disquieting recesses of my mind, shutting them off like a quarantined, plague-ridden area. The wall took years to build. It was always developing chinks or having its foundations washed away by emotion from the other side. But there seemed nothing to do but go on rebuilding and patching with the patience of desperation. Occasionally I tried to relax with alcohol. But I soon discovered that mine were not the sort of sorrows that could be drowned. And emerging from a period of drunkenness, I would find that my terrors were upon me again in intensified form. I sometimes went out walking, longingly eying the pretty girls I saw. On rare occasions I got up the courage to speak to one of them, and on the still rarer occasions when I was not rebuffed, I discovered that this act of speaking to strange attractive women on the street had an almost magical power to relieve my depression. At least it seemed magical to me then. I did not realize at the time that this was simply a form of masculine self-assertion, deeply needed by my disturbed, neurotic mind. But such encounters were infrequent, and seldom led anywhere. For the most part I still remained unacquainted with the people in the landscape. In time, as my methods of thought control brought me more success, I even began to take a perverse pride in my ability to thwart, outwit, and crush the gnawing animal. I pictured myself as an indomitable warrior fighting continuously against overwhelming odds, back to the wall. Few people, I imagined, had ever fought such a battle. I would never give up, no matter what the odds. Unfortunately, there was no other human being who could appreciate my heroism—or at least so I thought. I never dared mention my battle to anyone, for to mention it meant public admission of the existence of the gnawing animal—and to admit its existence meant to put myself at its mercy. I sometimes went out with friends socially. The gnawing animal was always with me. For hours at social gatherings I would put on an outward mask of serenity, attempting to hold a rational conversation while fighting the gnawing animal, not daring to give the slightest external sign of the battle. I attempted to give the appearance of a sane, well-balanced man. After several hours, having put up a serene front and convinced myself that people were accepting me as a normal person, I would feel that I had subdued the animal and would reach a temporary sense of relative security. The battle took a physical toll. I was thin and underweight. I also began developing serious stomach trouble which remained a chronic condition for nearly twenty-five years. But I had found a temporary, if painful, refuge in stoicism. I was, as the saying is, "beside myself." I would stand guard nearly twenty-four hours a day outside the prison of my other self, tensely watching for him to make the slightest move. He would menace me in a thousand ways. Always, in the end, I would club him into submission. "No matter what," I would say to myself, "I will not give in." And when I had finally convinced myself that I was the absolute master, I would feel relieved.

Actually, of course, the idea that there were two personalities involved in this queer business, was an illusion, or, to put it differently, a metaphor. The name of the gnawing animal or the "other self" was fear. Nevertheless this fear seemed to have many of the characteristics of a real person. He would lurk quietly until I was relaxed and vulnerable and then attack me suddenly. He would whisper to me insidiously, breaking down my reserve with suggestions that I was really weak and unable to cope with him. I could never find a moment of carefree spontaneity without becoming conscious immediately that he was at my elbow, ready to pounce. Even when I felt comparatively happy, I would have an arm raised, so to speak, to ward him off if he showed signs of plunging toward me. He closely resembled the childhood demon who used to suggest, "Wouldn't it be terrible if you saw a human skeleton seated in that chair?" (The skeleton always appeared.) I often referred to myself in the plural as "we" when thinking or talking to myself. I had the feeling of carrying another person around with me wherever I went. I was even humorously conscious of this curious situation, and I used to defy him with gestures and epithets. When he would awake me suddenly in the middle of the night with a terrific attack of panic, I would sit up on my bed and raise my fist or thumb my nose at him, saying aloud, "You think I'm afraid of you, you lousy bastard! Get back where you belong! No matter what you do to me, I am the master." In a queer, perverse way, these statements were inverted prayers. I was acting like a medieval monk exorcising the devil, except that I lacked faith in anything except my own stoicism. In the daytime I would feel the urge to make myself do things that I dreaded doing, just to prove that I could not only cope with my devil, but could also take him anywhere I wanted and fight him in any environment. If I was afraid to appear somewhere as a soloist, or make a speech, or deliver a lecture, or undertake a journey, I would deliberately force myself to assume the task. It would prove that I could not only do anything I pleased, but could fight him at the same time. I got a perverse pleasure out of doing things I was afraid to do, and carrying them out successfully in spite of him. When I had done them, carrying my devil on my back, I would feel superior to him and be able momentarily to cast him off. I seemed to get my greatest satisfactions from assuming tasks that terrified me, and I did them in a certain spirit of bravado.

I have noted somewhere earlier in this long manuscript that this particular breakdown seemed to involve a reversion to the habits of mind I had at about thirteen. The whole way of life that I had built for myself since that age—with its isolation, and its furious dedication to ambition—had collapsed. My great hope of impressing the rest of humanity as a genius had turned out to be a flop. My ambition to become a symphony conductor was completely thwarted. Miss Nesbitt—the lady whose image had inspired my battle against the windmills —had turned out to be a figment of my imagination. My subsequent marriage to a woman who was more like a mother than a wife to me had resulted in impotence and then in flight. I was back where I had started. There was, somewhere among the constellation of fears that made up the "gnawing animal," an aching void, a horrible sort of vacuum, that had once been filled by my mother and then by my wife. It was as though a supporting hand had been withdrawn, leaving me alone and helpless. Somehow that vacuum had to be filled, or

I had to learn to live with it. My ingrained habit of isolating myself from contact with other human beings had made it impossible for me to find the answer among my acquaintances. I had no real friends; all my acquaintances were casual ones. There was also a strong element of resentment involved in the constellation of fears. I resented the world for not being what I expected it to be. I had an angry irrational impulse to abolish the world of reality entirely—an impulse that was, in essence, suicidal. I resented the thwarting of my ambitions. I also resented—and perhaps this was the basic resentment —my failure to show myself as a man equal to other men. This particular resentment entailed that old fear of being feminine. Having failed at my ambitious plan to become superior to the rest of the world, I saw myself again as the helpless, lonely boy of thirteen, the boy who had been dominated by his mother, the boy who had been sent to dancing school, who had played the violin while his more normal colleagues had played baseball, who had never dared raise his hand aggressively against his fellows, and who had been ashamed of his slight, skinny, and rather delicate physique. All these things added up to a horrible fear that I was not a man, and, inferentially, that there was something female about me. My job, that of a violinist in an orchestra, seemed to me to be a female one. The violin had always been associated in my mind with my mother and with a certain lack of masculinity. It was a "sissy" instrument. Moreover there seemed to be something feminine about the position of an orchestra musician. The conductor seemed to be the symbol of the dominant male, playing upon the emotions and techniques of the musicians who were under him as if they were women. My entire reason for submitting to this profession of orchestra playing had been the hope that I might someday rise above it to become a conductor—a male. The ambition was no longer tenable, and I was left hopelessly trapped among the symbols of femininity. My feeling toward the orchestra was closely parallel to my childhood feelings of entrapment when I was forced to go to ballet school among throngs of girls. Somehow I had to get out. The violin was the symbol of my degradation. I must, at all costs, cease to be a violinist. Escape from my profession now became my dominant preoccupation. It was not easy. It took a long time. For three years more, I continued forcing myself to play as an orchestra musician, always seeking some way out. Finally, after a long struggle, including a great deal of severe economic hardship, I found another career. But before describing these events I must get back to my immediate narrative.

As I have already noted, I wore a broad-brimmed black hat, striped trousers, spats, and sideburns, and carried a cane. This eccentricity of dress was enough to stamp me as a foreigner in New York. I added to it a state of mind which I imagined to be European: I thought of Paris (where my family was still living) as home, *except when I was in Paris*; I looked down upon the cultural and artistic apathy of my fellow Americans; I found New York a hopelessly ugly and uninteresting city, and other American cities worse; I considered my country a cultural province of Europe, and I had an idea that anybody who was not interested in music was a philistine. I often visited Paris during the summer months. I was more European than American, or so I thought. All this until I found myself talking to my musician colleagues, who were only too enthusiastic about running down America. With them I would take the opposite point of view and become very angry, telling them that there were other things in the world besides music, that most musicians were ignoramuses, that they really knew nothing about America, and that it was a great country, far superior in many respects (if not musically) to the various countries of Europe. Any attack on musicians on the part of the outside world would cause my blood to boil in their defense; any attack on the outside world of America on the part of musicians would make my blood boil in defense of America. I appeared, in both states of mind, to be defending myself—for I was that curiously split creature, that contradiction in terms in those years, an American musician. I think I must have been fostering the illusion that I always had potential allies somewhere else, though I was invariably at the moment surrounded by potential enemies. As a musician I was a foreigner in America; as an American I was a foreigner in the musical world. I have since noted this peculiar habit of mind in other people, especially musicians, refugees, artists, and members of other minority groups. They are always desperately fighting their immediate associates and pretending to themselves that they are inhabitants of a different world where they have allies and people who love them. Put them in the different world and they reverse their field. Their allies, the people who love them, are always somewhere else. Their spectacular changes in love and hatred are amusing to watch. But they are really symptoms only of a dreadful feeling of insecurity, inferiority, and loneliness.

Though I looked like a foreign musician, and strove rather arrogantly to intensify this impression among my fellow Americans, I began to feel a strong necessity to learn about something besides music. I knew that people in the glamorous world outside the musical profession discussed things like politics, the theatre, the movies, and the doings of prominent personalities. I had tried feeling superior to these things in my lonely isolation as a potential musical genius. But since it was becoming painfully evident that I was not a genius, I wished to know something about what other people were interested in. I began systematically reading the newspapers—something I had never done before. I began developing opinions on political issues (before this I had always regarded politics as a vulgar and semi-criminal area. This attitude is not uncommon among musicians—especially Europeans who have been brought up in paternalistic societies). I began, for the first time, to get some inkling of the fact that commerce (or business) was not a shady, dastardly occupation carried on by professional cheats, but a necessary part of civilized society. I even began reading about murders and divorces. This was an imperfect world that was opening up to me—a far dirtier and noisier one than that inhabited by the ghost of Beethoven and the traditions of violin technique. But this rowdier world contained things I desperately desired—mainly the company of attractive women. I can now see through the illusion that caused my behavior. There were attractive women in the musical world too. But they never seemed attractive to me, because this was an area in which I had failed to become a man. I would read my favorite columnists in the newspapers with enormous romantic admiration. What men they were! They seemed able to write well on any subject, and their subjects included the whole range of normal human activity. To me, at the time, the humblest police reporter was a hero. He associated with dangerous characters—policemen, criminals, psychopaths, and other aggressive people who were not afraid to live, and were sometimes assertive enough even to commit murder. To my Casper Milquetoast mind even a murderer or rapist seemed a romantic figure. To have the courage and toughness to commit rape! It might be criminal, but it took a capacity for aggression that was sadly lacking in a person like me. *I* was afraid to *talk* to a strange girl, let alone rape her. The whole world portrayed in the newspapers which I read every day seemed to be a world of action, in which people strove fearlessly for what they wanted, and sometimes got it. The newspapermen who recorded this lively scene and seemed to understand its detail, became much more glamorous figures to me than Bach and Mozart. If only I had been a newspaper reporter instead of a musician. That was a man's job!

Meanwhile, as I have already noted, I had discovered that writing offered me a method of calming my terrors by enabling me to forget them temporarily. I soon began writing a book. It was a book on musical aesthetics. Writing about musical aesthetics was not as glamorous as writing about rape and murder. But at least it was writing. Perhaps it would entitle me to a sort of junior membership in the wonderful masculine company of writers. After all, if I wrote books I was entitled to call myself a writer. I didn't have to mention the shameful fact that I was writing about music. On the other hand, I did not dare to write about anything else. I knew a great deal about music, and felt secure in airing my opinions on the subject. Writing about anything else involved an element of risk. I might fail, and failure at this one method of escape from my entrapment as an orchestra musician was unthinkable. It would shatter me completely. So I wrote about music, still conscious that I was partially entrapped by the art, but thankful that, at least, I could call myself a writer. Nobody ever read the book I wrote. It was never published, and actually it was so sophomoric and naïve that I am glad it never saw print. It clarified certain ideas in my mind, however, and I learned something from it, both about writing and about musical aesthetics. When I started this book I was twenty-four, and obviously a very confused young man. When people asked me what I did for a living I said, of course, that I played in the orchestra, but quickly added, with pride, "I am a writer on the side. I am writing a book." The subject of the book I avoided mentioning if possible. I hoped that maybe they would think I was a novelist.

During these years, from time to time, I met and associated with a few literary people. My writer friend from San Francisco, Whit Burnett, who had followed me to Paris, subsequently turned up in New York as the publisher of a magazine devoted to fiction by budding authors. I saw him occasionally, and he invited me to literary gatherings where I met one or two writers of prominence. I was extremely diffident at these gatherings, anxious to be accepted but fearful that my subject (music) deprived me of full membership in the company of real writers. I admired the writers I met, at a distance, but I was unable to make any real personal contact with them because of my hopeless feeling of inferiority. My friend continually encouraged me to try my hand at fiction, and offered to publish whatever I wrote in his magazine. But two things prevented me from trying. I was too twisted psychologically to understand the most elementary features of human relationship—and these features are after all the stock in trade of a fiction writer. Second, he was always trying to get me to write a novel about musicians. I even tried this in a desultory sort of way. But it was impossible. My enormous resentment against music and musicians made me conceive the life of a musician as one of continuous martyrdom and humiliation from which any sane man would wish to escape. Several times I tried to lay out a novel on the subject. Always my hero was a man who regarded music as a dreadful trap and wanted desperately to escape from his profession. This did not add up to a novel about musicians. As a matter of fact most musicians did not act like that. I was the only musician I knew who hated music. Why couldn't I understand musicians well enough to write novels about them? I had lived among them for many years. But the block was always there. Try as I might, I couldn't write the novel. Something was wrong. Just what was wrong, I have only recently discovered. Music and the musical life were so confused in my mind with childhood humiliations that I was incapable of taking an objective view of them.

While my desire to write fiction was thus thwarted, I seemed to have an endless interest in absorbing and evolving philosophical ideas or concepts. It was not until a few years later that I discovered that my mind totally lacked the outlook of a fiction writer. I produced torsos of a couple of novels—poor ones. I thought that it would be nice to bask in the reputation of a novelist. But I was concealing from myself the fact that the process of trying to write fiction was, for me, not only difficult but boring. I simply didn't have the knack. On the other hand, I have always been one of that minority of people who read philosophy for stimulation and excitement. To me, it is no dry-as-dust subject, but an infinitely fascinating field of intellectual fantasy. I have heard it described by others (particularly young people just out of college) as a meaningless intellectual game of no significance in the modern world. I agree that it is a game, but *what* a game! I also think that practice in this game refines the intellectual capacities, and that the modern world is greatly impoverished because so few of its inhabitants are capable of systematic philosophical thought. But I shall not press this point here. I merely want to note that I have always read books on metaphysics, aesthetics, ethics, theology, and the critical study of history with the sense of suspense and stimulation that most people get out of detective stories. At the time of which I am writing I came across a book of this sort, which, for better or worse, had an enormous effect on my thinking for many years afterward. It was Oswald Spengler's *The Decline of the West*. Undoubtedly this brilliant and provocative but gloomy and hopeless book appealed to me in part because it gave a rationale to my resentment against the world I was living in. Spengler seemed to be agreeing with me that the world was in very bad shape indeed, and blamed this bad shape on a fatalistic (and very Germanic) theory of historical determinism in which I and all other men were depicted as helpless pebbles ground under the glacial sweep of time. Spengler's arguments were very convincing; doubly so to a musician whose education had been, in a sense, Germanic, since music had been for two hundred years very much a German art. Music itself was obviously in a state of decline. Contemporary composers had lost the art of writing great symphonies and operas. The "revolutionary" music of such men as Stravinsky, Berg, Webern, Schönberg, and their international imitators was very fashionable in "advanced" circles at the time. But to me, most of this music was superficial and emotionally meaningless. It seemed to represent a frightful decline from the great affirmative music of the nineteenth century, and this decline was quite logical when considered from Spengler's point of view. The Spenglerian attitude seemed to fit my pattern of conflicts and frustrations like a glove. It seemed to make logical my intense desire to escape from everything connected with the art of music. At the same time it developed in me an intense nostalgia for the nineteenth century. If I had only been born in the nineteenth century, I thought, I would have lived in a world where music was an important art, worthy of men of ambition like myself.

History and the decline of Western civilization had betrayed me. I was living in a century where the art I practiced was sinking like a leaky ship—a ship in which I appeared to be trapped.

My picture of the nineteenth century was heavily influenced by my long stay in Europe and constituted a romantic fantasy rather than a true appraisal. The civilization I had known in Paris and Vienna still retained strong vestiges of nineteenth-century habit. If I had remained in America during my formative years, I might have changed more easily in tune with the modern world which America represented. Instead I had, so to speak, made a three-year journey into the past and become hopelessly infected with a love of a world that was dead. I was thus, to a certain extent, a living anachronism. I did not seem to belong to the century I lived in. There was nothing about it that I liked. Yet I seemed to sense that the twentieth century was after all the real world, and that my love for the nineteenth century was something I must somehow rid myself of if I was to become a normal human being. The conflict was so strong that I insisted on dragging a vast weight of resentment into what should have been perfectly pleasurable aesthetic experiences. I could not listen to a piece of nineteenth-century music without feeling that, in enjoying it, I was entrapping myself in the past world that it represented, and rendering myself incapable of coping with the world I actually lived in. A Beethoven symphony or a Verdi opera would entrance me with its insidious beauty, and then I would awake from my trance with a sense of horror, feeling that I had been living in an unreal world, and that my stamina for maintaining my position in real life had somehow been weakened. I loved the past, as represented in its music; at the same time I hated the fact that I loved it. For my love for it was associated with a desperate fear that it would entrap me, isolate me from my fellow man, and increase whatever tendencies I had toward abnormality. I felt somehow that I must learn to decline with Spengler's West, to accept the world that had ceased to produce great symphonies. Yet I resented the decline as if it were a martyrdom inflicted on me personally. I seemed to be living in two irreconcilable worlds. Despite my insistence that I hated it, I loved music, but my love for the art seemed to be threatening to destroy me.

It is not difficult to see in this ambivalent attitude, a projection or elaboration of the fundamental emotional conflicts that I have already described as peculiar to my character. In some strange, rather vague symbolic way, music, the great symphonies, the wonderful creative atmosphere of the eighteenth- and nineteenth-century Europe, all represented the world dominated by my mother, the world of childhood humiliation, of fears of being feminine, of inadequacy and inability to fight and compete with my fellows. On the other hand, the rough, rowdy, "declined" world of the twentieth century in which I actually lived frightened me. I had no faith in my ability to cope with it. Yet I knew that I must learn to cope with it if I were to live as a normal human being, for only in this rowdy outer world could I find contact with my fellow man. It is curious how powerfully music was connected in my mind with inadequacy and isolation. I had many casual friendships with musicians, and I knew a number of women who were interested in music. But my musical friends seemed to me to be merely fellow outcasts—victims of an endangered world of illusion—and women who were interested in music were not women at all. They were apt to admire me for my qualities as a musician, that is, for my qualities of weakness, sensitivity, and femininity, and my inability to take an aggressive tone toward the world. That was not the kind of admiration I desired. That was the kind of admiration one got from one's mother. And the admiration of one's mother was a very dangerous thing. It was a betrayal. If only I could interest a woman who belonged to the "real" world—a gangster's girl, for example, or the chromium-plated mistress of a ruthless businessman such as I often saw depicted in the movies. But I seldom met such women, and when I did I was too shy to approach them. They remained, for me, idealized dreams.

Meanwhile I continued playing in the orchestra, harassed by attacks of stage fright and subject to violent fits of depression, loneliness, and resentment against my musician colleagues. Occasionally I found a woman and attempted to lose myself in a love affair. But my romantic ideas about love were at a low ebb, and I lacked the self-assurance that would have permitted me to act the role of a true male. Very early in this game I discovered that I dared not confide my misgivings and my neurotic troubles to any woman who attracted me. The moment I mentioned them I found that I was really admitting my fears of not being a normal male, and this immediately destroyed the possibility of a satisfactory sex relationship. If I confessed my weakness I was in the position of asking for pity—and pity was something I didn't want from a woman. It entailed the possibility of dependence, and dependence was that awful, weakening, and betraying relationship that I had had with my mother and later with Ellen Appleton. So I carefully concealed my fears from the girls I came in contact with. I made a continuous effort to act the part of a dominating and fearless masculine figure. Sometimes I even succeeded in deceiving myself. I had numerous affairs with women during this period, but my sexual behavior was so plagued by fear and

IN SPITE OF MYSELF

near-impotence that I seldom found it the source of much satisfaction. In a way I was applying in the sexual sphere the same technique of impersonation, of "going through the motions at any cost," that I had found necessary in other phases of life. Normal men had affairs with women. Ergo, if I was to carry out my impersonation of a normal man, I would have to have affairs with women whether I enjoyed them or not. I set about seduction methodically and with a heavy heart, without any feeling of friendship for my playmates, merely for the purpose of proving somehow that I could go through the motions associated with the idea of manhood. Often after a single seduction I would lose interest in the woman entirely and never see her again. None of the women seemed satisfactory to me. They refused to remain idealized romantic dreams. They became personalities. And personalities frightened me, since human contact involved understanding, and to understand me meant to penetrate my mask and discover the quivering, insecure, cowardly creature that I really was. Once they discovered that, pity might follow and, with pity, dependence —the same old circle that had betrayed me before. Above all, I wished to avoid sympathy from the opposite sex. My tortured ego could not withstand it. What a magnificent basis for love-making! Nobody was to be allowed to penetrate my outer impersonation. To the world, and to women, I was to remain a confident, heroic character, not the wormlike organism that I really felt myself to be. If the woman showed signs of seeing through my masquerade, I fled. Today I can remember little of my sexual escapades of this period. Only a few incidents, humiliating alike to the women and to myself, remain in my mind. I was always either prowling in search of sex, or fleeing from it in terror. Never, did it seem, could I be friends with an attractive woman. I can recall one example. Through an

artist friend who was also a scenic designer I came in contact
with a small amateur theatrical group in Greenwich Village,
and, for a time, did some musical arranging for them. In the
group were one or two women with whom I carried on a pla-
tonic friendship for a time, but sex was out of the question
with them—they did not attract me. There was, however, one
girl—I can call her Catherine, though that was not her real
name—who attracted me greatly. Catherine was in the position
of the troupe's leading lady. She was blond, rather pretty,
and had that quality of aloofness which pretty women sometimes possess and which I have always found challenging. As
leading lady, she played glamorous parts and was obviously
the sort of girl whom many men found attractive. This made
her irresistible, for if anything could prove that I was a man
among men, it would be the possession of a woman who was
admired by other men. So I began pursuing Catherine. She
was not very intelligent, in fact not intelligent enough to admire me for my musical accomplishments. That meant whatever admiration I managed to elicit from her would be limited
purely to my prowess as a male—and this was what I wanted.
After a short pursuit, Catherine, to my amazement, suc-
cumbed and invited me to her apartment. But once I was in
her apartment and she had offered herself to me, she became
a personality—actually, as I could see, a rather commonplace,
childish little girl of about twenty, divested for the moment
of the glamour of theatrical life, no longer aloof—on the contrary, frighteningly emotional and anxious to entrap me in a
real human relationship. I became fearful, awkward and reserved, impotent and anxious to flee. I made my excuses as
soon as I decently could, and left. I never saw her again except
once when I discovered her looking for me in the crowd at
the stage entrance of Carnegie Hall after a concert. She did

not see me, and I quickly melted into the crowd and left her where she was. I have often wondered how a woman feels after such an episode. Does she think, "I must have done something wrong to repel him so suddenly after his passionate pursuit"? or "What was it about me that he suddenly took a dislike to?" Is she hurt? Does she suffer? Does she conclude simply, "This man is mad," which is nearer the mark? The truth is, of course, that the man is pursuing a phantom—following the pattern that eighteenth- and nineteenth-century romantic authors like E. T. A. Hoffmann knew so well. It was not the woman who attracted him. It was a mirage composed of illusions—notions of theatrical glamour, conquest of unattainable perfection, of a dream woman—above all, the attempted satisfaction of a powerful hunger in the disturbed masculine ego.

It was, of course, inevitable that I should drift eventually into a more permanent sort of relationship, since I had, despite my fantastic attitude toward sex, a strong need for the companionship of a real woman. I found this companionship for a time with a woman whom I shall call Margaret. Margaret was somewhat older than I and a great deal more experienced in the ways of the world. I am afraid she understood me completely, and her understanding produced a feeling of inferiority on my part that ultimately led me to leave her. But she taught me a great deal. Margaret was at loose ends when I met her. She was a frustrated writer who earned her living as a stenographer, and inhabited the fringes of the Broadway Theatre, where a more successful sister was an actress of rising prominence. I knew the sister, whom I admired at a distance but who was much older than I was, married to a musician, and possessed of both fame and the sort of dominating personality that completely intimidates me in a woman. Margaret, on the other hand, regarded her sister with amused tolerance. Of the two, she was the more adult, the more worldly-wise, and the more balanced, if less gifted, personality. But she was not a success. She had, like me, come to New York from California.

Margaret was also a completely honest woman—perhaps the first I had ever met. She had a way of regarding me with critical detachment, undoubtedly seeing in me the child that I was, and weighing in her mind whether it would be wise to train me to blow my nose or not. She sensed what I needed, and also sensed, later on (though it hurt her), that she could not provide it. What she could provide was instruction for a very awkward young man in the art of love. When I first met her, her air of maturity and worldly wisdom interested me. But, as usual, my interest was strongly mixed with an element of rivalry. I believe my mind ran something like this: "This is a very sophisticated woman. If I can conquer her sexually, I will prove myself equally sophisticated, and the two of us can then look down on the rest of the world with the air of amused tolerance she seems to possess. I will then no longer be afraid of the world. I will be able to regard it with the cynical humor of a *boulevardier*." Since my only way of allaying my fear of a woman was to go to bed with her as soon as possible (thus, I thought, proving my superiority to, or equality with, her), I contrived to invite her to a little studio I inhabited in the upper stories of Carnegie Hall. I made a few preliminary conversational moves, trying to impress her with my brains and feeling quite ill at ease. She seemed impressed with my brains and discussed writing with me. Then, suddenly and very awkwardly, as if I were a man who had just made a decision to dive into a pool of ice-cold water, I pushed her down onto a couch and virtually forced her into having relations with me.

The act had about as much grace as a deliberate assault. She did not resist particularly, but she remained coldly staring at me with her big blue eyes, submitting with tolerant resignation but without enthusiasm. When it was over, she remained as unconquered as she had been before. Obviously I had committed a *faux pas*. This was not the way one approached sex with a sophisticated woman. My boyish ego remained unsatisfied. I had not conquered anything. I had merely proved myelf an awkward ignoramus. Up to then I had assumed that when you managed to make a woman submit to you sexually, you simply crowed like a rooster and thought what a fine fellow you were. This was clearly not the situation I found myself in. Margaret was not hostile; she was simply disappointed. I had gone about it in the wrong way.

I saw Margaret constantly after that for a period of several months. Her attitude toward me became deeply affectionate. Intellectually, we had a great deal in common. Both she and I had literary ambitions, and she seemed to respect the writing ability shown in the book and other manuscripts I was working on. My musical activity she viewed with tolerant interest, but, by some miracle, she never considered it to be the most interesting thing about me. She even regarded my exotic musical colleagues with amusement rather than awe. This was very gratifying. I had found a woman whose attitude toward the fact that I was a professional musician was neutral or indifferent, and who thought I had great talent for writing. To this extent, I felt, I was being admired for a masculine quality. On the sexual level, however, Margaret remained in the position of an instructress. This was not her fault—it was in the nature of things; she was much more experienced than I. But it put a subtle obstacle between us where sex was concerned. The obstacle was a slight wound to my self-esteem. It produced a feeling that I was again being dominated by a woman and put, so to speak, in the female rather than in the male position.

I gave in, in this relationship, sufficiently to learn for the first time that sex is a two-way concept involving tenderness and consideration as well as animal spirits. My twisted ego, which had rarely conceived either consideration or tenderness for another except in terms of taboos, fears of effeminacy, and feelings of guilt, badly needed the lesson. But the lesson could not be accepted completely without damaging my capacities for self-assertion. And, though on the surface I appeared to be a willing pupil, I resented my inferior status. This resentment expressed itself in a longing for a more innocent woman whom I could impress with my newly acquired knowledge. Though I never discussed this longing with Margaret, she divined it with a sure instinct. "Someday," she would say wistfully, "you are going to leave old Margaret for another woman. And you are going to be quite a man, thanks to what old Margaret has taught you." I, of course, protested this idea, and assured her of my undying devotion. But my protestations of eternal fidelity convinced neither Margaret nor me.

Margaret was, I suppose, another variety of the maternal woman. She seemed to take for granted the fact that ours was a temporary affair and that sooner or later I would leave her. She knew that she did not inspire me with enormous passion. She seemed to wish to leave her imprint on me (as indeed she did) as if I were a fine example of her handiwork—a "well brought up" lover, so to speak. She showed no jealousy whatever of other girls who might attract me. I remember once, at a party where we were both present, carrying on a mild flirtation with a very pretty girl. I later became conscious that Margaret was watching me. Afterward, she spoke to me, complimenting me on my technique, with pleased detachment as if I were a little boy who had just recited a piece she had taught me. Women are very mysterious. I know that Margaret had great affection for me; that she was conscious of being older; that she was, even when not in love, a big-hearted, generous woman; that she wanted desperately to have some purpose in life—preferably, I suppose, a child. Perhaps also she suffered from a feeling of inferiority which led her to accept the role of teacher (one can possess another a little by teaching him something for which he is grateful) rather than demanding full possession. Somewhere among these traits of character lay the explanation of her behavior.

On my side, I knew from the start that I was not in love with Margaret. And despite her extraordinary lack of possessiveness, I had a feeling of guilt because I did not love her. She seemed to be entrapping me with obligations toward her. I felt that I owed her a great deal, and that ultimately I was going to repay her by abandoning her. The specter that had always pursued me in my relations with women—the danger of entrapment by a new mother and the subsequent necessity of breaking free with all the attendant horror and self-condemnation because of the act—could be discerned even when I should have been happiest with her. I was never able to accept the blessings of day-to-day companionship without foreseeing the terror that lay ahead—the terror that I was going to leave her, and the opposite terror that I would not be able to leave her because of what I considered my great debt to her. My self-esteem as a man demanded a break for freedom and a conquest of a more feminine (or less motherly) woman. My sense of dependence, gratitude, and fair play seemed to make such a break unthinkable. I was not happy during my affair with Margaret. Whenever I left her to travel on tour with the orchestra, I became almost unbearably depressed. Even when I was with her, I was depressed because she knew too much about me, and made me feel like a child. I often confessed my neurotic fears and states of depression to her, and she would sympathize with me over them. But the sympathy merely depressed me further. This was not the answer. The masculine orientation that would have relieved my depression was impossible with her. I still did not feel like a man.

As I try to analyze this relationship from the point of view I had at the time, it seems that the thing that was most lacking in it was the element of idealization. (I was still seeking the sort of dream woman that I had pursued earlier.) It was impossible to idealize Margaret. She did not evoke the enshrined image that I had been accustomed to carrying in my mind during adolescence. She could not be transmuted into the powerful dream figment that Miss Nesbitt had been—the great female image which gave life its purpose and demanded absolute devotion in return. She was simply a friendly woman. She had no power to arouse the magic that my hunger for the unreal demanded. When I was with her, she soothed my fears like a mother. But when she was absent, the memory of her refused to serve as a talisman that would protect me. She lacked the characteristics of what I have called the "female icon." I was, at this time, frequently on long tours out of town with the orchestra. They were adventures in indescribable misery. For weeks, I would trudge with my musical colleagues from one small-town hotel to another, hopelessly alone, surrounded by people I had no intimate friendship with, conscious of a great gap in myself which could only be filled by the vision of a woman. And Margaret was not that woman. The most frightening symptom of my neurosis during this period was acute insomnia. I often went three nights running without closing my eyes, meanwhile dragging my weary body from concert hall to hotel to railroad station in an interminable trek, until sleep would finally come from complete physical exhaustion. The United States was then under the rule of prohibition, and I had not discovered the palliative effects of alcohol, used in moderation. I occasionally got drunk on bootleg liquor, and sometimes slept as a result. But on awakening, all my terrors would return. Many of my colleagues would spend nights in local houses of prostitution. But I had no heart for this sort of activity. I found prostitutes universally stupid and ugly, and I was afraid of them. I envied my colleagues their pleasure, but I was convinced that I was not one of them. Any participation in their homely habits seemed to me an unthinkable descent into a sordid life. I wanted no part of it. Isolated and miserable, I continued going through the motions. Back in New York, Margaret was waiting for me. But Margaret was merely another problem, not a solution.

VI

IV

During this part of my life—my affair with Margaret was an example of this—I was almost completely passive in sexual relationships. I told myself that I prowled in search of women, but in reality I usually attached myself to the nearest, most available and convenient woman, and remained attached until depression drove me off. There were exceptions, however, to this utter passivity. On one occasion, I actually managed to "pick up" a perfectly strange girl—one of those beautiful chimeras who pass one by on the street, remaining in the memory as infinitely desirable, possibly because one simply never gets acquainted with them as human beings. This girl had the round face and dark hair which, I can now see, reminded me of my aunt Caroline and my Mexican nurse. She was Italian by birth, but had been in America for a long time. She smiled easily and had beautiful teeth. She was very young—perhaps eighteen. I first saw her in a restaurant, eating with a group of other girls at a nearby table. She smiled in

my direction, and after looking behind me and assuring myself that the smile was intended for me, I smiled back. As she
left the place, I got up and followed. She was walking with
another girl, but soon the other girl left her, no doubt by pre-
arrangement. I continued following, my heart beating rapidly.
I came abreast of her in the middle of Seventh Avenue (then
a two-way street with only moderate traffic). I said timidly,
"You don't mind if I talk to you?" or something similarly halting. To my great surprise, she smiled at me again, easily, and
said, "It's nice to do something unconventional once in a
while, isn't it?" I had broken the barrier! It was possible to
communicate with the women of the outer world—the ones
you admired as they went by but never hoped to meet. Her
name, it turned out, was Cristina. She was, like Margaret, a
stenographer, but Cristina was a *professional* stenographer, or
secretary, with no higher ambitions whatever—one of those
competent, personable girls who act as receptionists, typists,
and general women of all work in the offices of businessmen.
She went to bed with me very soon after our initial meeting,
and continued seeing me at intervals over a period of several
months. She was a healthy, sweet-spirited girl with no apparent neuroses whatever. She took sex for what it was, and
enjoyed it. She did have a feeling, which she sometimes expressed, that she somehow belonged to a lower caste than I.
This had never occurred to me until she mentioned it. She apparently regarded me as belonging to some sort of Anglo-
Saxon aristocracy, while she was a mere immigrant. I would
never have countenanced this class distinction. But I suppose
that, in some unconscious way, it bolstered my self-esteem.
Cristina's mind was uncomplicated by the intellectual furniture that had made Margaret's a source of companionship and
a danger to a successful sexual relationship. She was entirely
feminine, entirely unintellectual—as far away from the ma-

ternal hobgoblin as it was possible to get. I would take her to dinner and to the movies from time to time. Her Latin beauty failed to fade on close contact. I remember a few peculiarities about her personality. She insisted on being sent flowers at regular intervals, as a sort of guarantee of continuing interest. She had two articles of apparel that she never took off, even in bed—her stockings and a gold cross that hung around her neck. Cristina had originally been a devout Catholic, and had spent her childhood in a convent.

Cristina was to play a rather important part in my life many years in the future. But, at the time, I am afraid I neglected her. She had been so easily accessible and remained so—a phone call would bring her to my apartment almost any evening—that I took her for granted. At some point, the phone calls ceased, and I did not see her for another fifteen years or so. Her exit from the scene marked the beginning of one of the most unsuccessful episodes of my adult life—and it took up a great part of that life. This was my second marriage.

Margaret had a younger friend—a dancer and an aspirant to the acting profession—who had been absent from New York for a couple of years on tour. Before her leave-taking, she had been in love with a fairly well-known writer. For all Margaret knew, she was still in love with him, though he had broken off their affair before she left. She was to arrive shortly, and Margaret—apparently sensing that her younger friend would find herself still spurned by the writer and in need of male companionship (also sensing that my own relations with *her* had long since run down)—began to create a romance in my mind about this absent, but soon-to-arrive, personage. She was, Margaret maintained, a beauty, with a rare sense of fantasy, a habitual air of melancholy which invited masculine comforting, and a delicacy of form and manner that were exceptional. Anyone but myself, I suppose,

would have adopted an attitude of extreme caution at these
expressions of friendly enthusiasm. Any sane person would
have waited to see. But here was a good example, again, of
my peculiar passivity and tendency to be guided by others. I
had married Ellen, my first wife, because she happened to be
in Vienna and because both her parents and mine had hinted
that such a marriage would be desirable. I had drifted into the
affair with Margaret because I had a slight acquaintance with
her older friend. To what extent are normal people guided
into marriage by this family—or I might say almost "official introduction"—sort of connection? A great many, I suppose. Yet
it has been my impression that the field of choice open to most
people is larger than mine was. Do not forget my isolation at
the time. I had not gone to college, where so many well-
brought-up young men find their mates. I had virtually no
friends in New York. The musicians I worked with constituted a group I was bent on escaping at all costs. The West
Coast was far behind me, and, worse, my mother lived there.
I was remarkably anti-social. My training as a potential "genius" had made me so. The amount of work it required had left
me little or no time for sociability, once I had left high school.
I was poor financially, since musicians, at that time, were an
exceedingly ill-paid lot. I was trapped in a small circle. I had
several acquaintances—among them a professor of physics at
Columbia University who had an interest in music. He was
married, and his home was a center of sociability for fellow
scientists, most of whose talk was over my head. I had deceived him several times by going to bed with his only-too-
willing wife—something generally treated with tolerance in
those scientific circles, but also something that disturbed my
sense of good taste. (It was part of my character that I could
go to bed with another man's wife secretly and find no fault
with my, or her, behavior. But to go to bed with another man's

wife in an atmosphere of serene tolerance, with her husband knowing perfectly well what was going on, struck me as somehow outrageous. Why was I outraged? The first thought that occurs to me in this connection is that there is something terribly bourgeois about condoned promiscuity, or, as one might call it, "planned infidelity." There is another thought that follows immediately: When promiscuity is condoned on the part of married couples, half of its attraction is lost. You are no longer deceiving anybody. The secret is open. It can be discussed, so to speak, in the family kitchen, and the wife's husband is a party to it. The betrayal—which, I am aware, the psychologists can trace to the childhood Oedipus complex—is no longer a betrayal. The infinite joy of sharing a guilty secret with only one other human being—one's mother in new guise, no doubt—is absent. I am afraid that I have retained this quaint attitude all my life. I disapprove, quite puritanically, of open promiscuity. But it is no crime, to me, to go to bed with another man's wife in secret. And if my wife were to go to bed with another man, I certainly should not like to be made aware of the fact.)

Moreover, this wish for secrecy where sexual affairs are concerned, descends, I am sure, from my unwillingness as an adolescent to permit my mother, or any other members of my family, to know anything about my romantic sexual encounters. My experience had been that my family might take a critical attitude. It had been of the highest importance to deceive them. And I found, later on, that this habit of secrecy exerted a powerful influence on all my affairs with women. It was at the bottom of my strong sexual urges toward attractive women who passed me in the street. I had not met them through any normal social channels. My feeling toward them was secret from them and from my closest acquaintances.

But I am getting off the track. I was, as I say, trapped in a very small circle. My only adventure outside it had been Cristina. When Margaret told me about her friend, whose name, by the way, shall be Geraldine—Jerry for short—I was entranced—almost hypnotized, in fact—even before I had met her. She was in the theatre—that most glamorous of places where practically all women are beautiful, or can be made to look beautiful. The promise of a friendly introduction awaited me. She had had a love affair with a writer—that most manly and experienced of professional archetypes. She was, in short, almost the ideal woman. The curious thing about all this is that I was not in the least disappointed when I met her. She was a small, delicate, oval-faced creature . . . But I am beginning to describe her, which, at this point is a grave mistake, for the truth is that I hadn't the slightest idea what she looked like or what her other characteristics may have been. I was overcome by my own inadequacy in dealing with this new apparition which had had the honor of having an affair with a writer. I was accepted readily enough as a lover, once the friendly introduction was over. Margaret generously faded away. She had had other plans anyhow, I imagine, and she soon afterward departed from New York. I was left with Jerry, who was nearer my own age and a fit subject for the projection of the idealized female icon of my imagination— the protecting religious, or quasi-religious figure which I had sought desperately since my first disillusion with my mother— that is to say, from the age of about four. It is curious that my icons, and my devils as well, have always been female. Jerry was fit material for the projection. She was reasonably pretty. She was feminine to the point of immediate submission. It never occurred to me that I was possibly being utilized as a convenient subject for a rebound from her affair with the writer. Perhaps that was not even the case. At any rate there was about a month of intoxicating sexual activity with a healthy partner, and a great deal of romancing on my part.

Then Jerry, who was devoted to her budding career as an actress, went on the road again, and I didn't see her for at least two years. We corresponded erratically—I wrote many more letters than she did. Always I assured her of my deep devotion. Thoughts of her kept away neurotic anxiety much as thoughts of Miss Nesbitt had ten years before. I was, I thought, in love with Jerry. I don't think that Jerry was in love with me, though she kept up just enough correspondence to show that she regarded me with favor. For me, she served the purpose of the female icon. But I was not faithful to her. I had numerous affairs with various women. None of them lasted, and none of them displaced the figure of Jerry from my mind. I realize, as I write this, that my behavior was very peculiar, as seen from any normal point of view. The need of the icon— the overwhelming need of the substitute mother, which had bedeviled so much of my past life—was still forceful, and Jerry —absent for so long a time—filled it. It is true that the icon faded a bit, but it was still powerful.

I had, a couple of years before, been taken from Damrosch's New York Symphony into the merged New York Philharmonic-Symphony (later simply the Philharmonic), which was under the conductorship of Willem Mengelberg and Arturo Toscanini—a promotion of a sort (the pay was a little higher and the musicians were a bit more skillful), but a promotion that, at first, meant little to me except that it guaranteed me a living. A little later, however, I had the experience of playing under Toscanini himself, and this was something that I was never to forget. I had worked under a considerable number of eminent conductors. A partial list, made up merely of those who come to mind at this writing, would include Hertz, Damrosch, Otto Klemperer, Fritz Busch, Wilhelm Furtwängler, Ossip Gabrilowitsch, Willem Mengelberg, Sir Thomas Beecham, Bruno Walter, and Clemens Krauss. A few conductors, I had found, were fakes; some, like Sir Thomas, were highly intelligent men; others, like Mengelberg, were master orchestral technicians; nearly all were supreme egotists. Of the lot I would describe as geniuses only Furtwängler and Toscanini. And while Furtwängler's genius was of a foggy, mystical Teutonic sort, Toscanini's was always on display—an incredibly subtle knowledge of the emotional states of orchestra musicians, a capacity to create crises which called for superhuman effort, an absolute familiarity with every nuance of each score in the classical symphonic repertory, and an imperial talent for leadership. I have written extensively about Toscanini in another book.* Since this is a personal memoir, I shall limit myself here to describing the effect he had on *me*. He was far beyond anything I had ever dreamed of in my childhood notions of what a conductor should be. Perhaps the most remarkable thing about him was his ability to make musicians forget themselves in what seemed to be the sacred process of converting the score of a masterpiece into sound. The knack was almost hypnotic. For all the terrors of my tortured ego, I found myself utterly without self-consciousness in Toscanini's rehearsals and performances. Something bigger demanded my utmost abilities. There was no time for thought about anything but the supreme necessity for transcending my normal talents in the service of the art of music. I played under Toscanini for two seasons, always admiring him at a distance. I toured Europe under his baton. Then I left the Philharmonic. I had no desire to continue as an orchestra musician under lesser maestros. I left of my own

* *Geniuses, Goddesses, and People,* E. P. Dutton & Co., Inc., 1949.

free will, and, as it turned out, at the most inauspicious possible moment.

This was the middle of the Depression of the nineteen thirties. I became one of the vast army of unemployed which was the most economically alarming feature of the period. I had decided that, no matter what, I would never play the violin again, and I took pride in being able to walk the streets without that violin case that had, for so many years, been the inescapable badge of my former profession. I had a dreadful time making any kind of living, but I cannot express the feeling of euphoria that I experienced at having left music behind me. At first it was not left behind entirely. For a short period I taught ear training and harmony in various settlement schools. I also had a few private pupils in composition—some of them kindly members of the orchestra who were concerned about my unemployed status. I knew what I was aiming at. I was going to become a writer. The trouble was that I didn't know anything to write about except music. For a time I became an assistant music critic on one of the New York dailies. At least I was sitting on the other side of the footlights. The pay was practically nominal—a tenth of what I had earned as a musician. But I was writing for a living. At one point, through an agent, I sold a series of four articles to a big national magazine. The articles were, of course, about music and musicians. I was paid what I considered to be astronomical fees. But I soon ran out of the sort of subject matter that was both musical and suitable for big-circulation magazines. There was nothing I could do but go on teaching and writing an occasional piece for the musical magazines, which didn't pay much. I had reverted to the bohemian life. I did my own cooking, and didn't get a great deal to eat. Restaurants were now way beyond my means, except for that blessed institution, the

Horn & Hardart automat. But the rigors of this life seemed a small price to pay for my release from the art in which I had once been a prodigy. That was, thank God, all behind me now. Even to be unemployed, or virtually unemployed, seemed somehow a blessing. The streets were full of the unemployed in those days. It was normal to be unemployed— much more normal than it was to play that fiddle. It was a second chance—almost a second birth. But there were problems.

One day as I was finishing a meager lunch I had got together in my apartment, there was a knock on the door. It was Jerry, returned from her years on the road, looking a little run down and carrying her worldly belongings in a suitcase. If I were writing in the vein of Henri Murger's *Scènes de la Vie de Bohème,* this would have been a rapturous occasion. But it was not. I looked carefully at my visitor. This was not the icon I had stored in my memory. This was a stranger, a woman obviously coming to me for refuge, but someone I had known very little of. I could remember the month of intoxication—with someone or other who had created a new icon in my mind. But I had not troubled, during that month, to really identify the object of my passion. I had had an affair not with a human being but with a chimera conjured up partly out of my own imagination. The real Jerry—the personality—had remained obscure to me, or perhaps it is more truthful to say that I had made hardly any effort to get into contact with it. I am aware that normal people pick their mates after a healthy friendship, dating them repeatedly while leaving other options open, and finally making their choice. At any rate, this is as it should be. But I was living in a world that I made up as I went along. It was an imaginary world in which I stood in direst need of the feminine icon. The women who filled it did not need to be examined as human beings. They were, in fact, not human beings at all, but fantasies attached to one woman or another who happened to enter my life at some point. And I clung to these fantasies as a monk clings to his crucifix. I had played, all over again, my experiences with Elaine Nesbitt, and had come to the same denouement. This was not the icon; this was somebody else. However, Jerry was the raw material from which the icon had been constructed. She was, moreover, a woman in distress, and Sir Walter Scott had long ago informed me that women in distress were the proper objects of knightly endeavor. I had pledged undying devotion. I had this pledge to redeem. And, again, my fidelity to Jerry as the icon had prevented me from making any serious connections with other women. Besides all this, I was lonely. So, apparently, was she. We were both almost at the end of our financial resources. Perhaps two could live almost as cheaply as one.

I invited her to share my apartment. We lived, to all intents and purposes, as man and wife. About ten years later we legalized our union before a judge. I felt neither one way or another about this ceremony. It was a matter of fate. Being the sort of man I was, I seemed doomed to this sort of relationship. Besides, how did I know? Perhaps all married people were caught up in similar circumstances. Or perhaps I—with my peculiar background—could expect only this situation as the best that was possible for me. Was it the best that was possible for her? I suspect not, but I have no way of knowing. A woman will sacrifice a good deal in order to assume the outward appearance of having a mate. I realize that I am not being clear. What I am trying to convey is that Jerry had become the friendly woman with whom sex was impossible for me—or rather that she slowly became that, following a period in which sex was at best a rather perfunctory thing. It never occurred to me to break the bonds that I myself had forged between myself and Jerry. That would have been the unthinkable thing—the betrayal of the substitute mother once she had been duly enthroned. Just how strong this feeling was in me will be further demonstrated in a later episode of this narrative. And, as I think back on the situation, it seems to me that the same thing would have happened with any woman, given the peculiarities of my own view of life. Any woman assuming an intimate relationship with me was doomed to misfortune. I was a poor risk as a husband; I was not capable of carrying on a successful life as a married partner. Elaine Nesbitt had been lucky to have been excluded from my life. Jerry was to be the real victim of my neurosis. There are women who would have sensed the situation correctly, walked out, and slammed the door in my face. Cristina was possibly one of them. But Jerry was not. Her nature was submissive and fatalistic.

For anyone else, Jerry would have been the ideal wife. She had many virtues—among them loyalty and the capacity to be a good sport. She had the "show must go on" discipline of the true professional, and she never gave in to small illnesses, or allowed fatigue or depression to interfere with her household duties. She was invariably sweet-tempered. She was self-effacing, and she knew enough about the artist's or writer's life to leave me strictly alone while I was working. She was extremely shy in society; so was I—and so we led practically no social life. She became a very good cook, and she took good care of the apartment. At one point she got a job with the W. P. A. Theatre Project which brought in about a hundred dollars a month—more than I was making. She was always there when I got home from an evening of concert reviewing

(I had an ill-paid job as a music critic for the Brooklyn *Eagle*), and she was always eager to consider my comfort. She was a good woman in the sense that she was always thoughtful and conscientious, and, if you consider things rationally, you might well ask what more on earth I expected, or wished for. It is a good question, and perhaps it is unanswerable. But I felt that I wanted to be in love with Jerry. I wanted Jerry to be something that she was not—the imaginary figure that I might have chosen freely, unhindered by my own neuroses. This was, of course, impossible. I had chosen a phantom that I had once known passionately for a few weeks. Had the real Jerry chosen me? And if so, out of what? Love, despair, the need for dependence? I do not know. Like most men in a similar situation, I felt that *I* had chosen *her,* and I experienced a great deal of guilt over the fact that I was not really fulfilling my duties as a married partner. I am not a God-fearing man, the church having been denied me along with society's other rituals. I have convinced myself that Christianity, like other religions, is more or less a matter of mythology. (I do not write this in a spirit of disparagement or condescension. In my view, it is very difficult for mankind to live successfully without myths.) But I used to pray before I went to bed every night, "God, make me love Jerry." A useless and preposterous request, of course. You cannot love another by an act of will, or by a divine dispensation either. Besides, what was this "love" I was asking for? A devotion to the female icon of my imagination, nothing more—a need, fostered in infancy, for the idealized substitute mother. "Idealized" is an important word here, for in reality Jerry was very much a substitute mother to me, and she was producing that sense of entrapment, that hunger for escape, that I had associated with my real mother. And what I was asking for, in addition to this, was to be absolved of all the problems created by my own irresolution. Being the kind of person I was, I could find no escape but this forlorn hope of a miraculously granted state of mind similar to that of my infantile sexual fantasies. Really a curious situation. Most men—or so I imagined—were held to a woman by passion or its embers, or, at the very least, by a deep friendship—sometimes, of course, by money. I alone among all the men in the world seemed to be held by a combination of infantile mother dependence and a sense of honor. And the sense of honor really boiled down to sheer egotism coupled with fear. Men of my special virtues, I thought, did not run away from helpless women. If they did, some colossal form of retribution awaited them, or something utterly terrible would happen to the woman. The latter had been the case in Puccini's *Madama Butterfly*. Most people would think this statement laughable. But consider my upbringing. *Madama Butterfly* was, like the novels of Sir Walter Scott, a part of my psychological conditioning. As far as I knew, these were models of real life.

As you can see, I was dismally unhappy and utterly frustrated. When I went out for a walk, or left town for a few days, the icon—the false Jerry—would return to my imagination and serve me as a talisman. When I returned home there would always await me, as if afresh, the discovery that the real Jerry was not the imaginary one. Here, again, was the stranger. I would take up my daily life as before, determined that my face would never betray the slightest hint of the disillusion that I felt. My face, too, had been trained by years of stoical behavior. If I had been a normal fellow . . . But what is the use of considering that alternative? The fact remains that I was not.

I do not wish to give the impression that my life with Jerry was entirely miserable. The unhappiness existed only in the realm of sexual frustration. We were good friends. We gave the impression, I think, of being an average married couple. She had, like me, been brought up in California, and we made numerous summer trips there, driving out by various routes. I myself made a trip to Peru to write some articles on the indigenous music of the Quechua Indians, and I was glad to get home after this, to me slightly frightening, venture high into the Andes. Our economic situation improved. I moved from the Brooklyn *Eagle* to Hearst's New York *American* with an enormous rise in salary, and from there to *Time* magazine with another boost in wages. We bought, and fixed up, a small hillbilly farm in Vermont, and spent some summers there. I began to go on trips in connection with my work for *Time*— to Hollywood, to Europe, and so on. Partly because of Jerry's shyness in society, partly because of my own habits of soli- tude, we seldom went out. And on my trips to Europe—some of them extended ones—Jerry did not wish to accompany me. She went instead to stay with her mother in Santa Barbara, or she remained at home awaiting my return.

My work, meanwhile, began to take on a much more satis- fying form. I had been hired by *Time* magazine as a writer on music. To my great delight, it was discovered some time after- ward that I knew too much about music to write about it with the "fresh approach" demanded by *Time*. They didn't need an expert there; they simply wanted a general writer. And so, for the first time, I began to write about other things—art in the beginning, and then nearly everything else.

My duties at *Time* magazine were peculiar, but I learned a great deal while performing them. My writing was sent on to editors who rewrote it completely, turned it into sausage meat, so to speak, and then stuffed it into the magazine. The kind of work this involved was rather hard on the ego of the writer who took his writing for the magazine as a serious artistic product, and there were many among the writers who complained bitterly about the editorial treatment their work received. At first, I, too, was caught up in this resentment. I did not really care what happened to my work at *Time*. But, as music writer, I was under the editorship of T. S. Matthews, a schoolmasterish fellow, a former poet and book reviewer, and a man who was not only tone deaf but, I think, slightly resentful of the prestige of an art that he had no way of understanding. Matthews had convinced Henry Luce, our leader, that what *Time* needed was an improvement in literary style, which could only be brought about by hiring more poets to write for it. He had hired a group of poets to work under him. Most of them were poor journalists, and some of them complained bitterly about prostituting their talents. But what with special conferences, dinners at Matthews' expense, and encouragement of all sorts, they managed. Matthews was engaged in the technique known on Madison Avenue as "empire building." The secret was to get a group of absolutely loyal followers and then, when a vacancy occurred in the upper ranks, to move into it with a compact political machine and take control. As usual, I was an outsider. I had had more journalistic experience than any of Matthews' poets, and I was not part of his group. Moreover, I was wise enough to see the game Matthews was playing. He professed literary idealism, but he was practicing power politics. I never really trusted Matthews, though years later, after some troubles of his own, he became more human and more friendly toward me. He rewrote my writing in such an absurd way—including the introduction of Elizabethan puns—that I was ashamed of it even in these surroundings. Then, there was my large knowledge of music to contend with. Thank God we had no by-lines. I was anonymous, at least to the general reader. But I soon found that discouragement was causing me to write badly. Matthews also discovered the bad writing and came within an inch of getting me fired. I found that I had friends, however. Mary Fraser, the wife of Dan Longwell, editor of *Life*, and herself a woman of remarkable capabilities who had often served as a substitute managing editor in crises, decided to take over the editorship of the art department and asked for me as art writer. At first, I felt rebellious at the idea of working for *Time*'s only woman editor. But Miss Fraser was a very special woman. She never offended my sense of masculinity; she praised me unreservedly; as *Time* editors went, she was extremely gentle—making a change only here and there. I was happy to be away from music. I was, thank God, writing about something else, and getting paid for it. I was a new man, and I think that *Time*'s art department profited.

The trick, of course, was to write about something you knew little or nothing about, but could bone up on in a hurry— one of the basic techniques of journalism. *Time* magazine was at the time, and no doubt still is, one of the most efficient machines for the production of news copy—written with a fair amount of depth—that has ever been created. In its offices, the subject of an article would be presented by the writer to the managing editor at a preliminary conference, and either accepted or rejected. If accepted, the subject would be passed on to one of an army of competent and attractive "researchers"—most of them Vassar, Wellesley, or Smith girls—who promptly set about digging up all the known facts about it, using as sources encyclopedias, specialized books, the incomparable *Time* morgue (or "library," as it was euphemistically called), the wire press services, and the newspapers. If nec-

essary, the researcher would interview personally anyone involved with the subject and write a complete report, with
quotations. A couple of days later all her material would be
placed on the writer's desk. He would then read through it,
digest its most suitable items, and write his piece. The piece
would then go to the departmental editor, who would cut, re-
write, and polish it, and then send it on to the managing editor, who might make a few small changes before putting it
into final form. It would then go back to the researcher, who
would check every word to be sure that every stated fact was
correct. Once corrected, it would go, with perhaps a cut or
two, to the printer. It will be noticed that, in this process,
the responsibilities of the writer were minimal. All he had to
do was string words together fairly acceptably. Whether they
were true or not was not his concern. Truth, or fact, was
solely the responsibility of the researcher. The ultimate style
which the words assumed was the responsibility of the editors.
This was a situation calculated to spoil good writers. But the
machine, grinding on week after week, was actually a fairly
efficient school of journalism.

At *Time* magazine, I began to make the first friends I had
ever had, aside from the reformed alcoholic, the Brahman,
and a few people in the music critic's profession, like Miles
Kastendieck, Louis Biancolli, Irving Kolodin, and Noel
Strauss of the *Times*. My colleagues were generally well-
scrubbed, handsome boys from the Ivy League universities,
and they accepted these writing jobs as their right. Very few
had been through the grubbier environment of the newspaper
business. None of them came from a background even remotely resembling mine. Many of them married pretty researchers and settled down to raise families in the suburbs.

There were a few, however, who did not fit this pattern.

One of them was James Agee, who since his death has been acclaimed as a writer of some consequence. Agee had had trouble with his mother too, and his reaction to it had been more overt than mine. He had been brought up by his mother to bathe regularly and to brush his teeth, so, as an adult, he seldom bathed or brushed his teeth. He refused to dress like the Ivy League boys, though he was, in fact, a Harvard man. He wore tennis shoes and often had holes in his pants. The advertising department, at one point, protested against his appearance, since he might be encountered by potential advertisers in the elevator. He was a sort of hippie a generation prior to the hippie era. His private life was amazingly disorderly. While he sympathized with the poor, he had no use whatever for communism, which was then a popular idea among the New York intelligentsia. He used to save up his pay checks without cashing them. He disliked the idea of income tax, and was often behind in his payments. On the other hand, Agee had an almost Christlike sympathy for all people. He could talk to a ditch digger with the same open, innocent camaraderie that he maintained with his fellow writers. He was a poet, but he was not one of T. S. Matthews' group. In fact, he disliked Matthews and always elaborately mispronounced his name as "Mathoos." Agee was potentially a great writer, and he was the only genius I can think of who was actually being dragged down by his menial work at *Time*. He disliked working for *Time*, but he had a wife and a new baby to support, and he was always giving away money to needy friends. He wrote beautifully for *Time*, only to see his writing put through the machine like that of the others. He found writing a slow and difficult business, and his handwriting was so small that you almost needed a magnifying glass to read it. If I remember correctly, he never used a typewriter. His work was typed up later. For several years Agee occupied the office next to mine. On one side of his desk stood a bottle of whiskey; on the other a bottle of benzedrine tablets (then a newly discovered stimulant). He would tank up on whiskey while he was writing until the point was reached where he could no longer concentrate. Then he would take benzedrine to sober up, reach the point of concentration again, and remain there until he felt he needed more whiskey—and so on back and forth. Actually Agee was methodically committing suicide. Later, he went to Hollywood, where he worked on a number of movie scripts for John Huston, playing tennis meanwhile in spite of a weak heart. Ultimately, back in New York, he died in a taxi.

Another prominent exception to the prevailing Ivy League type among the writers was Whittaker Chambers, who arrived on the staff shortly after the Hitler-Stalin pact. Chambers had, of course, been a communist courier, and had just broken with the party to become one of its bitterest enemies. He was a short, plump man with bad teeth, who contrasted mightily with the rest of the staff. He was also secretive, and conspiratorial-looking. On the inside of his jacket he carried a large hunting knife for protection against what was then the equivalent of the NKVD. He seriously expected to be assassinated. One of his close friends, in fact, *was* assassinated—or so Chambers believed, on fairly convincing grounds. This was General Krivitzky, the anti-communist Russian who was found dead in a Washington hotel room under suspicious circumstances. Chambers wrote foreign news articles, and then was promoted to be a department editor. He became a very close friend of mine, and we used to eat lunch regularly together at Billy the Oysterman's, a since defunct restaurant across the street from our building—often in company with Wilder Hobson, Herbert Solow, Walker Evans, the photographer, and Jim Agee, all of them members of the staff at the time. Chambers always sat with his back to a wall. He was a widely read, highly intelligent man, and a good writer. He was also capable of humor, but not about his past or the Communist Party. If such subjects came up, a veil of secrecy would fall and he would become uncommunicative. Chambers was undoubtedly a rather fanatical fellow. He had had all the fanaticism it takes to be an active communist and participant in the party machinery. Once he had broken with the party, he pursued anti-communism with the same fanaticism. Undoubtedly he knew more about what was going on in communist circles than the rest of us did, and his feelings on the subject were probably well founded. I did not enter into this phase of his life. Outside it, I found him a highly articulate man, with interests in things like German literature (which was a blank to my Ivy League colleagues), Greek and Thomist philosophy, history, and many other subjects. I saw nothing to account for the pathological accusations that were made against him by the psychoanalyst Carl Binger later at the Hiss-Chambers trial. Hiss was, I suspect, not only a victim of Chambers but also a victim of history. A time when it was heroic to be a communist (the Roosevelt era) had been succeeded by a time when communism was regarded, even by the intelligentsia, as a dubious business; and Russia had changed overnight from a place where an interesting social experiment was being carried out to a possible powerful military opponent. Once involved in the case, Chambers was forced to play it out like a Greek tragedy. The only gainer in this trial was the then Senator Richard Nixon, whose political stock began to soar. I have always had to protect Chambers' reputation from the assaults of my liberal friends. Whatever he did, I am positive that it was in a spirit of righteousness, driven by genuine fears for his country.

Wilder Hobson, who had succeeded Matthews as editor of the cultural departments when Matthews rose to be managing editor, was also one of the more interesting members of the staff—an unsuccessful novelist, a man who twice left *Time* Inc.—finally for a job as book reviewer for *Newsweek*—a veteran of psychoanalysis, an exceptionally gifted raconteur, a pretty heavy drinker, and a person capable of occasional fits of rage, always over real injustice of some sort. He was extremely sensitive to music, and for a time under his editorship I returned to the music desk, where I found my work under him quite painless. He was also a wonderful companion. So were Herbert Solow, an ex-Trotskyite, a man of gentle humor and almost saintly character, and Walker Evans, a great artist photographer who was then writing the art column, and whose rather Edwardian temperament and continual dry witticisms were a source of entertainment to all of us.

Life at the office, at this time, was pleasant enough. But I was being galled somewhat by my anonymity. If I troubled to write well, I wanted my name attached to what I had done. For a time, I fed this hunger for recognition by writing articles for other magazines, most notably the *American Mercury*, which was then being edited by Eugene Lyons. But since I was still known primarily as a musical expert, all the articles of this sort that I wrote concerned music. This was an unsatisfactory situation. Meanwhile I had been called up by the draft for the Second World War, but was deferred on grounds of health. Actually I was perfectly healthy, but a tendency toward nervous intestinal spasms evidently made me unfit. I was also rather old; I had just passed forty. In 1941, taking advantage of the scarcity of writers, I applied for a transfer to *Life* magazine, of which my friend Dan Longwell, Mary Fraser's husband, was editor. *Life* had, in its upper echelons, a group of men who were known as "senior writers." They included John Chamberlain, Charles J. V. Murphy, Noel Busch, and Robert Coughlan—all well-known journalists—and they wrote articles at the heads of which their names were printed in large type. I suppose that my longing for a large by-line and the public acclaim that I imagined went with it was childish, but I wanted to be one of them. At first I was simply an all-purpose writer, doing texts for those absurd items entitled "*Life* Goes to a Party" and similar things at which I became fairly expert. Then I became movie editor—an agreeable job entailing occasional trips to Hollywood and, at home, screen-ings of five or six movies a week from which I picked one to review, in picture and caption style, as "Movie of the Week." Longwell allowed me, from time to time, to branch out into more ambitious projects, and after a few years I became, in due course, a senior writer. *Life*'s senior writers, in those days, occupied a pinnacle of a sort in the journalistic profession. They were paid better than any other writers except certain columnists and the roving correspondents of the *Reader's Di-gest;* they could pick their subjects; they had practically un-limited travel allowances, and there were those great big by-lines. This was success of a sort, and about as far away from music as you could get. I never had to write about mu-sicians, though I did turn in, and see published, a few articles on musical personalities like Toscanini, Artur Rubinstein, and Ezio Pinza. My field stretched all the way from satire and humor to movie personalities, reports from abroad, and po-litical pieces. *Life* published practically everything I wrote, and the *Reader's Digest* picked up at least half of it. Longwell was gradually retiring, and giving place to a younger editor named Joe Thorndike with whom my relations were equally cordial. Thorndike sent me to India for six months to observe the sociology, politics, and religion of the place and to do, among other things, an article on Jawarharlal Nehru, who was then Prime Minister. My *Life* connections gave me entry almost everywhere. I found India utterly fascinating, and Prime Minister Nehru quite cooperative. I traveled over practically every region of the big subcontinent, and I wrote the pieces I had set out to write. I returned to America with a severe case of infectious hepatitis, but this belongs to a subsequent part of my narrative.

Jerry, as I have noted, did not accompany me on any of my trips abroad. She did not wish to, and our married life was becoming a series of interludes between separations. While I ransacked Europe from Finland to Italy in the immediate postwar period (the war was over, but the occupation was still in force in Italy and Germany, and I wore a U. S. Army uniform with a shoulder patch that read, ironically, "War Correspondent"), Jerry went, for a period of nearly two years, to live with her mother in Santa Barbara. Our marriage had not been really successful, owing entirely to my own neuroses. As with my prolonged connections with other women, sex had died out completely after a couple of years, and a terrible sense of confinement had followed. Obviously, I was simply not a marriageable man. I could not be true to a woman with whom I lived in intimacy. I was untrue to Jerry several times—once or twice with her knowledge; but this was not satisfactory either. My deceptions were done with a dreadful sense of guilt. Then, there was a long period of complete sexual abstinence. To me, marriage meant impotence and a feeling of entrapment. There seemed to be no way out. But at this point a new interest entered my life. I rediscovered Cristina, or rather she rediscovered me. I had written a book that was reviewed in the newspapers, and the reviews told Cristina where to reach me. I had not seen her for nearly fifteen years.

VII

The thing grew gradually, and I was hardly aware of its existence until it was upon me with overwhelming force. It was the only substantial love affair I had ever had with a woman, and it was a peculiar, limited love affair, carried on in secret and having no domestic attributes. It lasted for ten years, during most of which time I was married to Jerry. Jerry, as I have noted, was often absent. I myself was absent from time to time too. But the minute I returned, I got in touch with Cristina, whom I saw virtually every day while I was in New York and to whom I wrote continuously while I was abroad. Whether Jerry suspected anything, I do not know. I think she may have suspected, while refusing to recognize her suspicions. Or maybe she realized that our marriage was, by this time, held together very tenuously, and wished to give me freedom, though not the freedom of complete separation. Cristina this time appeared in my life in a decisive way. I asked her to lunch. She did not, at first, appear terribly attractive to me. I had long since forgotten the little eighteen-year-old who had been my companion before I had taken up with Jerry. Cristina was now a woman. She had drifted here and there, always supporting herself respectably by her work as a secretary, and had finally married a salesman. Their marriage had not been happy. The salesman had gone downhill, lost his job, and become a hopeless alcoholic. Every evening she would search the neighboring bars, and even the sidewalks and gutters, to locate him and bring him home to bed. He was totally dependent on her, not only emotionally, but, at the time I met her again, financially too. Cristina was supporting him on her small salary and trying to make a home for him and keep him more or less in it. They had had no intimacies of any sort for years. He would start to drink the moment he waked up in the morning, and would continue, in semi-dazed condition throughout the day, slipping off toward evening to the muddled sociability of various saloons from which he would finally emerge practically unable to walk. Cristina's marriage was obviously unhappy, but like many strong characters in unhappy marriages, she was doing her best to keep this one going—at least to outward appearances. When I had first taken her to lunch, I was not, as I have said, immediately attracted to her as a woman, but I found a certain agreeable companionship in her company. We had known each other long ago. There was a good deal to talk about. Inhibitions kept me from disclosing the problems of my own life with Jerry, but Cristina, who was pretty shrewd in matters of the world, must have made a guess or two concerning them. I found myself dropping into the habit of lunching with her every day. After a week or so, I broached a proposal: Why didn't we go somewhere where we could be in private and take up where we had left off a decade or so before. Cristina nodded enthusiastic approval. The only place in mid-Manhattan to go for such clandestine purposes—unless you are a millionaire and own several apartments—is a hotel room. This may seem sordid to the conventional reader. I assure you there was nothing sordid about it. New York contains many nice hotels, and many of them are used for honeymoons. It is only necessary, for an affair of this kind, to fill a suitcase full of books or other fairly weighty articles, walk up to the desk clerk confidently, sign a fictitious name with a Mr. and Mrs. in front of it along with a fictitious out-of-town address, to have privacy in any first-class hotel in New York. You go home after your intimacies, and return next morning to reclaim your suitcase full of books, which, of course, is kept locked. Naturally, you have to change first-class hotels continuously so that you will not be recognized. But New York has an inexhaustible supply of them. In the course of the next few years, I came to know intimately the insides of countless hotels in New York—one of the few important cities whose hotels I had never been acquainted with. Since I was now relatively well off, the expense of this sort of thing could be easily afforded. Cristina was the same in that she never removed her cross or her stockings, but she was different in some other respects. Her figure had filled out into that of a woman who might have tempted a sculptor. She still had that lovely smile, round face, and dark hair. She approached sex with what I have often imagined to be a typically Latin earnestness and solemnity—as if it were a sacred rite encompassing a tragic truth of some sort. I grew more and more fond of her. I saw her every day at lunch. She exacted flowers as before. I made her presents of clothes, going with her to the department stores to help pick them out. Cristina became a very beautiful woman, and not just because of the clothes and other things that I bought for her. She blossomed again, I think, because there was now something in her life that she could be happy about.

I, too, had something to be happy about, and I looked forward to each meeting as something around which my life revolved. I was, however, subject to certain feelings of guilt. I overcame them by drinking a good deal, though I never slipped over the edge into alcoholism. The routine was much the same when I was in New York: The morning was devoted to work at the office. Then lunch with Cristina. Back to the office again until about five—and if it was a "hotel evening," then there was a drink or so at a pleasant bar, and a signing in, with that trusty suitcase full of books, at one of New York's better hotels. I had telephoned home to let Jerry know that the pressure of office work demanded my presence until later that night. Cristina and I would go to dinner at some restaurant, and then I would take her home. By a coincidence, she lived just around the corner. As I have said, I did a good deal of drinking. It did not in any way impede my sexual activity; in fact it had the opposite effect of releasing my inhibitions and quieting, for the moment, my feelings of guilt. Never in my life had I imagined myself so adept at sex. My sex life had never been particularly satisfactory. Now it was phenomenally successful. Coitus could be prolonged as much as a half hour with all sorts of tender endearments expressed in the process. I had never been as close to any woman, except possibly my mother—and Cristina was my mother's opposite—a dark Latin woman reminding me unconsciously of my benevolent aunt Caroline or of the Mexican nurse I had had when I was an infant.

As I try to analyze the exceptional nature of this affair with Cristina, certain points concerning it stand out. It was, as I have said, sexually successful beyond my wildest dreams.

Why, aside from Cristina's attraction, should it have been so? I had known, and gone to bed with, attractive women before, but never with such gratifying results. The answer, I think, is that this was a totally secret, a hermetically sealed, affair. Cristina was as unsullied by normal social contacts as if she had occupied the retort of a medieval alchemist. She knew none of my friends. I had met a few of hers, but this had been seldom, and I never made close acquaintances among them. Thus, she did not participate in any part of my normal social life, nor did I in hers. Nobody was in a position to criticize our relationship, or even comment on it, because nobody knew about it. It existed outside all social formality, outside society itself. My mother never would have approved of it; society wouldn't have approved either. I was escaping them all. I had finally found, in the flesh, the dream woman—the woman you admired while passing her in the street, knowing that you would never meet her socially. Cristina answered to my most secret desires. She was not subject to the stresses and disillusions that, to me, accompanied all affairs that were polluted by public sanction or common friendships. It was a unique situation—or so I thought in my neurotic way. I had a beautiful creature in a glass case. If the glass were broken and the outside world let in, I knew very well that the whole thing would be ruined. And if it required a certain amount of alcohol to sustain this unique situation, that was a small price to pay.

Or am I reading a point of personal eccentricity into what is a fairly common procedure? The French and Italians, wise in matters of sex, have built a whole system of marital and sexual relations on a psychological basis that is not so different from this one. Marriage, to them, having been sanctified by the Catholic Church, is a sacred union—a union aimed primarily at the begetting of children and at family stability.

But their system has always allowed for secret sexual outlets, and clandestine affairs have become, for them, not only a pleasant social convention but also a staple feature of their literature.

Of course, there was always the problem of homecoming. I would conceal, as best I could, my delight. I would be slightly drunk. I may have smelled of Cristina's perfume. Jerry said nothing in any case. One of Jerry's outstanding virtues was patience. She welcomed me home as if I were tired after a strenuous day at the office. I tried my best to look tired, instead of inspired to the point of walking on clouds. Usually I would retire to the living room, where (of all things) I would play *music*—records on the phonograph. Something mysterious had happened here. I rarely went to hear music any more. I had convinced myself that my past life had led me to dislike it. Perhaps these clandestine meetings with Cristina were gestures of defiance at my mother. They had removed the curse of my childhood and exempted music from my catalogue of fears. Curiously, the music I played was invariably that of the operas of Richard Wagner. No, not *Tristan und Isolde*, as you have guessed, but the *Ring* cycle. And I played these operas loud enough to wake the neighbors, had there been any neighbors to wake (our apartment was unusually situated next to a building whose inhabitants were always away, and above another apartment inhabited by an old, deaf couple who liked what little they could hear). Was this a pagan ritual? A defiance of my former fears? I do not know. But it was a celebration of a sort that never would have occurred to me since the time I had abdicated from music. I was no longer afraid of entanglement with the art. I could love it, or love some features of it, again. What Jerry thought of the sudden appearances of these musical orgies, I have little idea. I imagine that she blotted out all suspicion from her mind and concluded simply that I was tired and drunk, and satisfied herself with that explanation, since any other would lead to trouble. My sexual relations with Jerry had, of course, long ago come to the point of complete cessation. She accepted this with her customary outward show of patience and forbearance. We continued to live together as if nothing out of the ordinary was happening.

It will be obvious to you that my marriage to Jerry had, by this time, become a mere formality. But it was not obvious to me, or, I think, to Jerry. Though it grated on my nerves and made me feel guilty because of my infidelities, it still had a peculiar hold on my emotions. Jerry still had enough of the charisma of the mother image to make the thought of leaving her inconceivable. Had it come to a showdown, I would have remained with her and dropped my affair with Cristina. Jerry was still my responsibility, and though I knew only the pleasures of friendship with her, I still regarded myself as bound to her for life. This was not because of any religious ideas about the sanctity of marriage. The bond arose, if my analysis is correct, from the following sources: first, of course, the status of a substitute mother that I had endowed her with. Second, my own exaggerated self-esteem—conscientious men like me did not go back on their word, and when they pledged devotion to a woman, the pledge stood. To break the pledge would be to admit that I was a less admirable creature than I imagined myself to be. Sir Walter Scott would not have approved. Third, Jerry's own obvious helplessness—or what I conceived to be her helplessness. Here again my self-esteem was involved—how could she possibly get on without me? And she was fulfilling her part of the bargain by being the patient, long-suffering, uncomplaining wife. Also, of course, there was a certain inertia. I was now comparatively happy, owing to Cristina. Why disturb things? Then, there were my long absences from home, and Jerry's long absences visiting her mother. During the former, I was lonely not for Jerry but for Cristina. During the latter, I was delighted to live alone. I imagine that Cristina, though she was not particularly neurotic, felt herself to be in the same boat. It would have taken a lot to make her leave her alcoholic husband. Not as much, perhaps, as it would have taken me to leave Jerry, but a good deal nevertheless. And Cristina, too, seemed happy with things as they were. People who are authorities in such matters have since pointed out to me that my relationship with Cristina was by no means a complete one. It involved none of the responsibilities of marriage. Its moments of companionship were intermittent, and ethically forbidden. Was it not the very fact that Cristina and I were *not* married, and secretly in love, that led to all this happiness? Probably so. Marriage to Cristina would have involved many things that had no place in our relationship—the feeling of entrapment, the dull day-to-day routine at home, and above all, the creation of a social milieu which would have killed the ecstatic quality of the affair. I cannot imagine a married couple—and I don't believe such a couple exists—which could sustain, over a long period, the passionate feeling Cristina and I had for each other. It was a special sort of union, something preserved *in vacuo,* which could be indulged in at will and then put back on the shelf again. It was not a complete relationship, and it indicated perhaps that I, as a male, had not arrived at a point where I could accept a complete relationship. At any rate, that was the diagnosis of the experts. Nevertheless, I am glad that it took place, complete or no. I still cannot see it other than as an unparalleled experience, destined for

me alone, because I was the sort of man I was and had suffered enough to entitle me to it. Do not forget that I was already into my late thirties when the affair began. My prior
life I would willingly consign to a junk heap. Nothing on
earth could persuade me to live it over again. It amuses me
when people say, "Ah youth!" or, "Oh, to be young again!"
Perhaps others are really, honestly, looking back to what,
for them, were happy years. For me, they were, on the whole,
an unmixed horror. For me, life—as the saying is—began
at forty, or in the early forties. But there were things radically
wrong with it even then.

For a long time I refused to even think about my marriage
as something that could be continued or dissolved. But one
day—I was by this time about forty-five—I came to entertain
the honest thought that I wanted to leave Jerry forever. My
prayers to the God I didn't believe in appeared again, and
this time they were, "Please God, let me find some way of
getting my freedom." The prayer was ultimately answered.
But let me stop for a moment to consider its peculiar nature.
I was, in effect, again asking to be absolved of the consequences of my own irresolution. I could no more have faced
Jerry and asked for a divorce than I could have scaled a prison
wall. The very idea of leaving her seemed to be a betrayal of
my responsibilities. It was the unthinkable thought. I thought
it at night when I went to bed—drunk, for, as I have noted,
I had by this time taken to a considerable amount of drinking
in order to dampen my conflicts and get to sleep. In the morning I would swallow the thought down and pretend that it
didn't exist, going on about my work and my meetings with
Cristina. But the thought was present all the time.

A number of things happened at this time to precipitate a
crisis. I had been on my long assignment in India—six months

of observing, interviewing, and reporting. I had been taken
ill there with infectious hepatitis, as I later learned. All that
I knew was that I was dragging along through my duties
with a curious feeling of lassitude. Having all my life been
subject to neurotic feelings, I naturally attributed my lassitude to mental causes, and dismissed it from my mind as much
as possible. I held myself on a tight rein. The territory I was
visiting was not the most pleasant in the world, though, to
me, it was endlessly interesting. It abounded with much more
serious diseases than hepatitis—bubonic plague, cholera, and
various tropical fevers. I was completely alone, except for
passing contacts with colleagues—correspondents of the press.
I did my work, and, at sundown, like the typical British colo-
nial, I drank until bedtime—which, of course, was not exactly a cure for hepatitis. After I got back, I was examined by
competent physicians and sent to a hospital where, by a long
rest, I seem to have overcome the disease. Out of the hospital
again, I resumed my work and my meetings with Cristina. But,
at home, anxiety began to rise in unquenchable form. I had
to find some way of leaving Jerry; the idea of leaving Jerry
was unthinkable. These were the irreconcilable points that
were contributing to the anxiety. To make things worse, Mr.
Shawn of *The New Yorker* magazine made me that very attractive offer if I would become its music critic. After a month
or so, I began showing signs of depression. I could no longer
write. I gave up the critic's job. It had only increased my misery by getting me involved, for a short time, in music again.
Or was the explanation different? Causes of given effects are
difficult to identify in any circumstances. For a man in a state
of desperation, they are doubly so. I was suffering from anxiety, but what, precisely, is anxiety? Mine, at times, felt like
uncontrollable rage. My face would flush and my heartbeat

quicken. I would have a feeling of pressure in the chest, as if my lungs were going to burst. This feeling of rage was accompanied by a feeling of fear—sheer terror. Of what? I did not know. If I tried to write, I would be overcome with fear. There were even physical symptoms, such as swelling of the hands. Most terrible was the thought that I was partially insane, and that there was no way for me to get out of my predicament. To spend one's life in that state was unthinkable. Suicide would be far preferable. Still, I desired to go on living. I would lie in my bed in a small room in the apartment staring at the ceiling. It was white, and there were cracks in the paint. It had not been painted for a long time. At my left, as I lay on my back, was a clock. Somehow that clock seemed important. It was a sort of testimony that I still existed, since it was the first thing I saw on awakening. Beyond it, at one side of the room was the desk at which I wrote. I could no longer bear to sit at it, but as long as I remained in bed I could look at it in a detached way. Causes? I went over and over them for an explanation of my condition. How did I get that way? The trouble with causes is that they are always multiple. I tried to distinguish some of them. My unhappy marriage to Jerry was one thread that led to my condition. But there were others. Infectious hepatitis, I knew, often left a residue of mental upset—exactly the sort of mental upset that I was experiencing. Was my condition the result of overwork, as well it might be? Or of a feeling of unworthiness, and the necessity for perfection, in writing for *The New Yorker?* Or of a recurrence of my association with music? Was I the victim of some mental weakness that laid me open to such attacks? (As you possibly remember, I had previously experienced a similar attack.) And if so, what was it in my nature, what debility, that made me prone to these attacks and what were *its* causes?

Childhood fears? I remembered my early dependence on my mother, coupled with my dislike of any intimacy with her and my hatred of the sort of childhood she had imposed upon me. But my mother had long since ceased to play any part in my life. I could remember easily the state of mental good health I had enjoyed prior to the attack. I had always had a sunny disposition, when normal, and everybody knew me to be a happy, humorous sort of fellow. There had been a gradual decline into the state in which I found myself. But the crisis had struck suddenly while Jerry and I had been at a small dinner party with friends. I had drunk whiskey after whiskey, and returned home in a state of drunkenness. But the alcohol had not relieved my depression, or anger, or whatever it was, and I hadn't slept that night. I called Mr. Shawn at *The New Yorker*, and told him that I couldn't go on with my music criticism. Soon, I could not cross the street without overwhelming fear. Now, I could not even get out of the house, where I was trapped with Jerry. I could not see Cristina. I could not even get out of bed except for momentary, anxiety-ridden trips to a nearby couch. Drink helped to quiet me so that I could eat, and barbiturates guaranteed me some sleep. But I was again in the grip of a breakdown like the one I had experienced before, and this time it seemed hardly worth the effort to adopt harsh stoicism as a remedy. It had been tried. It had worked for a while. But ultimately it had failed, as witness my plight of the moment. I sought out a psychiatrist, and my narrative has now come full circle.

Or, at least, it has almost come full circle. I have yet to come to the workings of psychiatry on the main problem—my wish to be free of my marriage at any cost. It took nearly two years of psychoanalysis before I could even bring the problem to the point of conscious formulation. My attitude toward

Jerry had gradually changed. I was now able to show my real feelings, and I had become a truculent, moody husband instead of the polite and patient one I had been theretofore. For the first time, I was able to scold her occasionally, poor woman. But facing the problem of a separation was a far more formidable undertaking. I had confessed to my psychiatrist that the one thing I most desired was to dissolve my marriage. But it took a long time before I could nerve myself to make the move. You are probably a normal person, and it will not be evident to you why this was such an overwhelming step to me unless you consider the kind of neurotic I was. By this time I had solved the work problem and was back at the office of *Life* magazine doing my daily job of writing. But the problem of Jerry was still with me. Then, one day, I nerved myself to tell Jerry we had to separate for a while. I meant to say permanently, but I was not equal to that. Jerry was to go to live in a separate apartment. I would send her money regularly. I am sure that Jerry, who knew well the peculiar lives that artists and bohemians led, and knew also that I was in bad mental condition, took me literally and assumed that the separation was to be a temporary matter. I had not been able to be honest with her. Nevertheless, on the day when she left, I came very near to suicide—I do not mean suicidal thoughts; I mean the act itself. I was terrified and anxious. But, above all, I felt guilty. Next day at the psychiatrist's I said, "I have killed my best, in fact my only, friend. I am thinking of doing away with myself." At this point the psychiatrist became aggressive and, for once, dropping his usual habit of passive listening, scolded me as he would a child. I was assured that I had just taken a great progressive step which I would never regret. Since, by now, I had considerable faith in him, I accepted this statement, though it was a matter of weeks before

I could climb out of the pit of depression into which the act had thrown me.

When I climbed out I telephoned Jerry and told her that we could not live together any more. She visited me shortly afterward to get the last of her belongings. Fortunately she departed quickly without prolonged recriminations. Later on, she left town and went to live with her mother. If I had been a stronger, more decisive man, with a greater knowledge of the world, the separation would have occurred fifteen years earlier—or the permanent liaison would never have gotten started. What a dreadful waste of two people's lives had been involved! And what a brutal separation had ended the affair and the marriage! No regrets on my part really. Only a boundless feeling of guilt. On her part, what? Perhaps more. I suspect that the blow to her was mainly the feeling of utter failure in what she had made a life career, and the terrible thought of personal inadequacy to life's challenges. But for me to survive, it was necessary to take the step. I am, of course, writing of purely emotional matters. Financially, I continued to support Jerry. Later there was a legal divorce in which Jerry received the proper alimony settlement.

Now, it will probably occur to you that this was a peculiar separation. Most men leave their wives for another woman. I had left mine simply for freedom. I would never have been able to leave Jerry for another woman, because of some absurd notion that such an event would have humiliated her more than the sort of separation I achieved. Actually, it was probably the other way around. I had left her in order to gain my liberty, and, as I saw it at the time, in order to recover from a crippling neurotic state. Why could I not have left her for another woman? This is a question that I cannot answer, but I daresay it has something to do with the betrayal of the mother image. One could leave one's mother, but one could not set up a rival mother with one's mother's knowledge and then leave one's mother for the other one. All my childhood romances, remember, were secret from my mother. One thing is certain. I did not leave Jerry for Cristina. Cristina did not understand the situation very well, or perhaps she understood it only too well on a practical level. She knew that my wife had left me. She noted that I did not make overtures to her immediately. She gave me back a small endowment insurance policy in which I had named her as beneficiary. In return she wanted a thousand dollars to get a divorce from her alcoholic husband. I was just recovering from a dazed condition in which I had been for some time, when Cristina telephoned me and informed me that she had married again. Curiously, I was not felled by this blow. I wished her well. Ours had apparently been, in some ways at least, a healthy relationship. It could be broken off without guilt, without any psychological complexities, with only a slight feeling of regret, and with many pleasant memories. Besides, it was Cristina who was doing the breaking. And she was a stronger person in such matters than I, or a more realistic one, which comes to the same thing. I could easily sustain the regret of being left by a woman. What I had found almost impossibly difficult was to leave one of my own volition.

Jerry's absence and Cristina's marriage had, however, left me in a strange position. For the first time in my life—or so it seemed—I was without a woman, and this was a disconcerting, not to say terrifying, plight for me. Would I ever be able to get a woman again? My psychiatrist assured me that I would. Meanwhile, he was my only intimate friend. I lived absolutely alone for several months, now consumed by doubts of whether I was attractive enough to women to secure an-

other partner. You will by this time have perceived that this
question was of crucial importance to me. I could not live
without having a woman as a wife, mistress, talisman, or whatever. I had always been afraid of attractive women and of
women who are beauties in the glamorous public sense. For
a short time I relapsed into my former habit of attaching myself to the most convenient or available woman—in this case
a girl whose husband had left her and who lived in a neighboring apartment. But I was now wise enough to see that the
old machinery was operating, and that this was not enough.
I had to change my habits.

All my life I have been regarded by my friends as an in-
veterate womanizer. In one sense this is true. I cannot live
without women. But in another sense—that which concerns
the joyful, heedless Don Juan—I was a bust, and my numerous
affairs, except for the one with Cristina, had generally been
unsatisfactory to the woman as well as to me. At this point,
however, I embarked on the life that, had I been a normal
man, I would have led in my twenties. With the utmost de-
liberation, I set about the pursuit of very attractive women,
steeling myself against rebuffs (I had experienced only one
rebuff before, at the hands of Margaret Anglin's soubrette),
and proceeding with great tenacity of purpose. I had developed an insatiable hunger for women—the prettiest ones I
could find—and I was determined to feed this hunger. God
knows, I was acquainted with scores of attractive women.
The trick was to go to bed with them. I was surprised at the
facility with which this could be accomplished, and for about
five years I became a gay bachelor, dating a variety of women
and taking a good many of them to bed. I was surprised at my
own ability at seduction. I was also surprised that the most
beautiful women could be seduced easily—often more easily

than the plain ones. I also discovered that beauty, in the
official glamorous sense, is not synonymous with attractive-
ness, that beautiful women are often sexually cold, that official public beauties are often highly neurotic and lead very
unhappy lives, while their attractive, but less beautiful, sisters
have, as a rule, a much better time of it. I began to apply a
maxim I had learned many years before—I think it was
written by a Frenchman: "If you want to succeed with a
woman, praise her for those virtues which she most conspicuously lacks." I solemnly declared myself overwhelmingly impressed by the intellectual faculties of a number of rather
unintelligent women who had the beauty of movie actresses.
They fell into my arms. Only I really understood them. Always polygamous by some strange instinct—I think it is an
instinct like a miser's—you cannot have too much of the stuff
around, and it would be terrible to run short—I often had two
lady loves at the same time, each secret from the other. If this
seems shameful, I can plead that I never had that freedom
and spirit of sexual adventure in my twenties when most men
have them. I was making up for lost time.

The women I seduced and sometimes lived with for short
periods, did not, to my surprise, take their affairs with me
terribly seriously. It seems that they were all quite accustomed
to affairs, and breaking them off when the time came was no
great problem. Generally one let them down easily, seeing
them less and less frequently until the point of separation was
almost undiscernible. I shall not bore you with a complete
account of my five years as a Don Juan, happy and adventurous though they were. But there were a few women with
whom I had affairs who were interesting enough as personalities to be worth describing. I was, of course, not invariably successful. There was one beauty whom I pursued

with every blandishment for a period of weeks without getting anywhere. I took her places, entertained her, tried to interest her in myself, but she would not be seduced. She claimed to have had an affair with, and to be still in love with, a Balkan terrorist she had met in Europe. Later I learned how to deal with this masochistic type of woman and her admiration for force. You use force. You turn her over your knee and spank her. But I did not know this at that stage, and so, after a few conventional efforts at seduction, I gave up and looked elsewhere. No use wasting time at the age I had arrived at.

There was an artist with a very sweet personality, beautiful in the movie-actress sense, not, however, overwhelmingly attractive to me, though I carried on with her for several months. There was an exceedingly pretty divorcée who took my praise of her brains literally. She already had a terribly high opinion of those brains anyhow, and used to argue with me heatedly about aesthetics and politics. She was an extreme conservative in the latter and thought she was a master of the former, though she really had little understanding of it. Her arguments, or one might call them lectures, were carried on with tense assurance. She was a terribly neurotic woman with unsolved childhood problems that were obvious to anyone with the slightest acquaintance with psychological theory. I could not keep up this relationship, possibly because she was always wounding my ego. There was a society girl, not, strictly speaking, terribly pretty except for a magnificent figure. I found her extremely attractive, and our intimacies were very enjoyable. She started out by going to bed with me but permitting no sexual contact. She also had a peculiar habit of trying to make me jealous by going out with other men and telling me about it. I suspected the sadomasochist type, and spanked her. After that all went swimmingly. I even took her along on a journalistic assignment in Southeast Asia. But basically she was a girl for whom society with a capital S was life itself. She was wealthy and spent a small fortune every month on clothes. Her life was one round of parties, and the parties were always with diplomats or members of the social register. I didn't fit into this scene, and, after almost a year, I abdicated, though much of our affair had been very pleasant. She made no fuss over the separation. She disappeared from my environment as smilingly as she had entered it.

The most interesting of these women though—interesting because of circumstances rather than personality—was the wife of a very peculiar man, an aggressive fellow who got most of his pleasure from holding sexual orgies at his home. He held a position of some authority in the advertising business. He seemed to have been deeply struck by Cecil de Mille's Rome. He invited large groups of young and handsome people to his home, cooked dinner for them, and then, playing Stravinsky's *Sacre du Printemps* on the phonograph, invited the whole assembly to undress and indulge in wholesale and indiscriminate sexual intercourse. The reigning queen of these festivities was his wife—I shall call her Felice—and he took great pleasure in watching her as various male guests carried on intercourse with her. Afterward he would take her upstairs to a bedroom and have intercourse with her himself. Felice was beautiful in a primitive way, exuding animal magnetism to an extraordinary degree, and I am sure that no male ever found it difficult to approach her with sex in mind. Like most women of her type, she thought she had a deep need to be really understood as a person. Her husband, though, had established a peculiar standard of morality in the midst of this Gomorrah he had created. It was all right for her to have intercourse with other men in his presence, but secret affairs were taboo. I was introduced to this couple by a mutual friend who didn't have the slightest idea what was going on. I found Felice very attractive and made a play for her. She visited me secretly in my apartment, which was nearby, and we began an affair. I, too, had had no idea what was going on. She confessed it all to me and wept. Now, this was a very bizarre situation. I had slept with other men's wives before, but not with wives who were being shared with every Tom, Dick, and Harry. I felt I had to have exclusive rights, and I deplored the orgies. She said she would face up to her husband and have them stopped. He roared like a wounded tiger at this suggestion, she told me. He said that she was making him impotent, since his potency depended on the orgiastic rites. By this time my vanity was involved. I set out to be the Galahad who would rescue her from her horrible fate. I proposed to marry her in order to effect this rescue. It was the last time I ever made use of the sexual principles preached by Sir Walter Scott. I visited her home from time to time. The husband, who had been duly informed of our affair and wish to be married, was furious. He roared at me, and he was a large man at least twice my size. We had several encounters. I was afraid of him. But I have discovered that when I am truly afraid, I adopt, almost instinctively, an air of complete calm. Felice took this calm for indifference and complained that I was not sympathetic enough to her husband's grief. Apparently, he thought of himself as an elderly man married to a young girl who was likely to deceive him, and the orgies were partly motivated by a desire to let her have complete sexual freedom, but with his knowledge. As I explained earlier, this sort of planned infidelity has always been obnoxious to me. The husband tried his best to be the sophisticated, tolerant man that was his ideal. He continued inviting me to the house. But when I got there he would become furious, break glassware and dishes, and curse me. There were times when I fully expected a knife or a revolver to end my life. I now regret the whole episode, for reasons that I shall explain. Felice was not intelligent enough to be a companion for me. Wit slid off her like water off a duck's back. She simply didn't understand it. I took her to the theatre a couple of times, and sat secretly taken aback at her reactions—mainly her lack of humor. Nor was I the sort of sexual athlete who could have satisfied such a woman. But I was dead set on getting her out of those orgies. Basically, I suppose, I have a puritanical mind. I was doing something for her own good. I arranged for a divorce between her and her husband. I sent her to the Virgin Islands for a period at considerable expense. She got the divorce, but she did not come back to *me*. She met another fellow in the Virgin Islands. When she got back she married *him*. He was another orgiast. I was deeply humiliated. All my Galahad gestures had been futile, and I had gotten sufficiently attached to Felice to feel that I had been jilted in a great romance. It took me several months to recover. As for Felice, she had shown a certain animal wisdom. She knew herself. And she knew that we could not possibly be compatible. At this point I also learned another thing. Felice, who was about thirty-four, considered me to be old. I was now nearly fifty. Her husband had been in his sixties. She had used me to get her divorce and then had married a man of about her own age. It was the first time anybody had referred to me as "old." That was something to think about. And afterward I felt sorry over the whole episode. A similar calamity probably would have happened anyhow where she and her husband were concerned, but I grew to feel sorry for him. In his way he had been in love with her.

He was a sort of monster. But that was his way of life, and I had destroyed it, to no purpose. Actually he was a rather interesting man, with a wide variety of cultural concerns and a habit of stepping aggressively into any business or political situation and making his presence felt. Under other circumstances I could have been his friend.

My life, during these years, of course, had become wildly social. I went to parties and I gave them. The purpose of all this activity was simply to meet and entertain attractive women. Old friends were rather taken aback to find my solitary and scholarly nature suddenly transformed. At one party in my apartment, given for about fifty people, several of them, including Wilder Hobson and a few others along with their wives, were very useful to me without my knowledge and against what were then my inclinations. Felice, the orgy girl, was present, and I explained to everybody that I was going to marry her. To my face, they were all complimentary and enthusiastic, but I noticed that Felice soon disappeared into the kitchen and refused to emerge. My friends, as I learned later, decided that Felice simply wouldn't do. She was not intelligent enough. That night, after my other guests had left, I had a big row with Felice. She had felt the snub while I had been quite unaware of it. She was not sexually responsive. I was angry, and I felt humiliated. In retrospect, I think that it was this occasion that led Felice to drop the whole idea of marrying me, though she afterward used my help in order to divorce her husband.

Ultimately, being the kind of man that I am, I sought out a serious partner for marriage. The role of a gay bachelor had become a bit strenuous for a fifty-year-old man, and I knew very well that I didn't want to continue this party-going life forever. I had completed what was merely a phase. I had demonstrated that I could bring to bed a considerable variety of beautiful women, and my ego, or my need for sexual self-assurance, had been satisfied. Now, I could embark on a more sober venture. And with a psychiatrist behind me, the fears attendant on such a venture could be minimized. What I needed was somebody to come home to, somebody who attracted me, somebody intelligent who could share ideas with me, and somebody with whom I would enjoy going out socially. It had taken me thirty years of adult life, two nervous breakdowns, and three years of psychotherapy to find out what I wanted. Even when I found her and actually married her, fears that she would assume the character of the old mother image sent me back to the psychiatrist again for a few post-graduate sessions. But she never did assume that character, nor did she take on the peculiar imaginary function I have referred to as the "icon." She has a round face like my aunt Caroline, my Mexican nurse, and Cristina. She is dark like them. What there are of her neuroses fit what are left of mine. I am, finally, at the age of fifty-two, a happily married man and—believe it or not—a joyful monogamist.

Not that I have been completely transformed by psychoanalysis into a perfectly normal fellow. I don't believe that anyone ever is. And I have known many people who have submitted to psychoanalysis for years apparently without any particular success. It just happened that I turned out to be a nearly perfect subject for this sort of therapy, and that I had an extremely skillful and sympathetic therapist. I am happy in my present marriage and happy in my work. It is true that a small residue of neurosis remains. I am still an insomniac, and I take barbiturates, much to the distress of my doctor. I also have several highly eccentric waking fantasies. One of these is that I used to cover the distance between my onetime home on Beekman Place and my *Life* magazine office at Rockefeller Center by running rapidly on my toes like a hundred-yard-dash man. This is patently absurd, and yet I have a vivid memory of it. Another fantasy is that by placing my feet at a certain angle, like skis, I can slide down any staircase with the greatest of ease. I never try this. But I am positive that I can do it, and I remember very well having done it many times in the past. Moreover, the general outlines of my character have not changed much. I am still a scholar by temperament; I am still somewhat anti-social, and I much prefer reading or writing in solitude to associating with people. I still refer to myself as "we" when I am alone, talking to myself. Fortunately, my wife has a sense of humor, and so there is little friction between us. As to the "real" world, I still have some suspicions that it is a dream from which I may someday awake, but I now know something about its rules, and I manage to get along in it quite well.

21 DAY BOOK